MY RACKET, HOW IT WORKED OUT

RAY ALLEN

America Star Books

First printing

eBook 9781611026269
Softcover 9781630845391
PUBLISHED BY AMERICA STAR BOOKS, LLLP
www.americastarbooks.com

Printed in the United States of America

JEAN

Thanks for being our
friend

Ray & Ann 2014

This book is dedicated to our grandchildren.
Michael Dean Cranwell
Rebecca Allen Cranwell
Katelyn Hope Forbish
Jennifer Marie Allen
Matthew Reid Allen

ACKNOWLEDGMENTS

First I would like to thank those around the world who have read my first four books. Your kind words and letters have kept me writing. I am always happy to hear from you. Feel free to contact me by email raymondfallen@cs.com. When you email, please identify yourself as a reader. I will do my best to reply.

When you have a spelling disability as I do, those who read and make corrections are of tremendous help. I thank each of you from the bottom of my heart. My Florida fishing partner and friend, Norm Lane, and his wife, Dean, were the first to correct my mistakes. Then Norm's sister, Elizabeth, and her husband, Walter Pish, were my second proof readers. These two couples improved the manuscript greatly.

Then all three of my children read it and made suggestions. Thank you for your help and the great joy it has been to be your father.

My youngest daughter, Katie, again has been my editor. She has corrected and improved the sentences in this book. Her daughter, Katelyn, scanned and sized the pictures for the book. Katie's husband, Larry, was the final proof reader.

I am grateful to my colleagues in ministry who have written their thoughts on this book, Dr. Tom Reynolds and Dr. Bill Ross, both who served on the staff at Blacksburg and Dr. Tommy McDearis, my successor at Blacksburg Baptist who has led the church in dynamic ministries. One could not ask for a more gifted or supportive friend than Tommy. Dr. Kunjamon Chacko has been a great partner in India missions and an inspiring friend.

Chubby Wiggins has kept my computer virus free and quickly solved any problems I have had with it.

I want to thank all the people at America Star Books for all you did to make *Light from the East* a success and publishing this book.

Last but not least I thank by wife, Ann, for 56 years of marriage for her faith in me, her help with this book, and her support and encouragement through the years.

Many unnamed people have helped with the work. I and I alone am responsible for any errors in the book. Where a story might reflect negatively on an individual the names are fictitious and the story modified so the persons cannot be identified. For security reasons none of the real names of military personnel are their actual names.

Ray Allen, Vinton, VA April 2014

FOREWORD

Dr. Tom Reynolds Retired Senior Pastor, Harrisonburg Baptist Church and Former Associate Pastor Blacksburg Baptist Church

When Ray's manuscript arrived I was about two-thirds through the reading of one of John Grisham's books. After reading the first few pages of Ray's book I was so captivated that I set the Grisham book aside. The problem was that it caused me to miss my afternoon naps on Saturday and Sunday as I had difficulty laying it down. In these pages Ray captures the excitement and adventure of a life committed to following God's unfolding purposes. His journey of faith is biblical in its dimensions. The telling of it is vintage Ray Allen—honest, bold and straight-forward.

Having shared ministry with Ray for eight years in Blacksburg, I got to know him well. More than anything else I found in him something pretty rare among Baptist pastors—authenticity. What you saw was what he was, inside and out. Some found this offensive. I found it refreshing. Ray provided for me the image of a the kind of pastor I would like to be—one who is true to himself and his vision of what God is calling him to be and do. He was encouraging and supportive of me when, after twenty years as an associate in three different churches, I felt the call to pastoral ministry. I have little doubt that had it not been for him I would not have spent the "second half" of my ministry as a pastor.

Ray liked to remind me from time to time that I graded his papers in the sole church music class he took at the Southern Baptist Seminary. It was a class required and almost universally despised by the ministerial students. When Ray took it I happened to be the student assistant to the dean of the School of Church Music who taught the class. Ray says I "gave him an 'A'." That's not so; he earned it. The class required no special musical skills. It was designed to be an introduction to church music class for future pastors in the hope that they would be supportive of the ministry of music in their churches. At that time neither Ray nor I imagined that I would one day be plying my trade, in part, as an Associate Pastor under his pastoral leadership.

As I read this account of Ray and Ann's journey of faith and practice from Amherst County, Virginia to far-flung parts of the world, I was reminded again of the Apostle Paul's words in Second Corinthians, "we have this treasure in earthen jars." Ray makes no pretense of being better or more gifted than other ministers. He has always seen himself as a regular guy that God has used to do some remarkable things. He learned early on that hard work, respect for authority and a high regard for those for whom he is responsible will get one a long way in any field of endeavor. I know this for I experienced it through those eight fulfilling years of ministry with him. As you read this book be assured that it is not fiction; it's real stuff—the stuff that makes pastoral ministry exciting and enduring.

One of the things I learned most from Ray, in terms of pastoral leadership, is not mentioned in this book. It consisted of an aphorism that he used often—"Tell the truth and trust the people." That stuck with me. I saw him do it often in the rare atmosphere of a university church setting in which most of the members were experts on something. Things could get pretty contentious there (as he indicates in the section on his years as Pastor of the Blacksburg Baptist Church). But in the midst of conflict he would write a letter, make a visit or call a meeting of key leaders and cast a vision of the way through the confusion. And when the chips were down he would call on the congregation for the final decision and it worked. A Baptist pastor cannot serve a church full of highly educated members as long as he did if he does not "tell the truth and trust the people."

Many of Ray's stories in this book moved me personally. I will cite two that demonstrate for me the reason that Ray has enjoycd the success that he has—his ability to see things in unique and creative ways and his willingness to risk failure. The first is his account of visiting the office of "James Herriot's" vet clinic. I, also, once stood before that same red door and it did not enter my mind to knock on it and risk disturbing the famous doctor. Ray knocked and enjoyed a delightful visit of more than an hour with him.

The second story is the one that touched me most—the gift of a cane. Ray refers to it at the end of his story. His reflections demonstrate his ability to see and articulate meaning in simple things. In this case a wooden cane that was too long to fit into his suitcase becomes a metaphor for living outside the box. As he puts it, "God is forever calling us to leave our boxes of comfort and step out in faith to walk with Him." By the grace of God Ray learned to live outside the box and we who have known him well are the better for it.

TABLE OF CONTENTS

INTRODUCTION DR. K. CHACKO, PRESIDENT, INDIA BAPTIST THEOLOGICAL

Dr. Ray Allen has recorded his biography and sent me the draft to write this introduction. We know each other and our families for over a period of 30 years. I read the manuscript of my friend telling his story.

Some lives are lived for themselves, and they do not make any difference in anybody. Others leave their foot-prints, influence other lives who impact others with the motivation received.

This biography has informed me, influenced me, and inspired me. Any person who will read this book will get his attitude changed, will move from the negative valley to the positive hill top. They will see his or her own life and will never be the same. The book will widen one's vision, enlarge his territory and deepen his commitment in the field of his/her profession. Ray has taught me his first principle of success. At titude+Dream+Discipline=Success.

The situation, however, poor or rich is not going to decide the destination. Anything is possible, but it may be difficult. Realistic goals are within our reachability. His first book *How To Be a Christian Happy and Successful* has touched my life, and I took his permission to translate into Malayalam and that book has helped many people to travel through the paths of life to victory. We preached together in many places in India in conventions, campaigns and revivals.

Ray and his devoted wife, Ann, have been our very good family friends in our good times and difficult times in the U.S. and in India. In 30 years Ray has visited India over 20 times. When I asked him the most fascinating thing in India for him, he answered, "The People."

While reading the book, I see Ray's earlier years—the most difficult ones. His struggles strengthened him instead of weakening. The military experience taught him discipline which is evident in all his actions and approaches. Experience in Sears, I will say, gave him the management expertise and public relations skill. Ray develops friendships with people at all levels.

Dr. Allen's life took a different turn when the Allens chose to go to seminary and later chose pastoral ministry. As a family, we consider the Allens as a model. Ray loves his children; he has time for every church member in their ups and downs. He was available to people. Ray has hundreds of friends in different countries in the world. He is a man you can trust. He appreciates people and gives them credit for their accomplishments. With his Pastorate at B.B.C., he showed the church what the world is and what the needs are. He moved the church to in-depth missions. India is one beneficiary. Ray laid the foundation of India Baptist Theological Seminary, and it was dedicated in the year 2000. So far 285 have graduated with Master of Divinity and Master of Theology degrees and serve as Christian ministers. He also helped us to establish the Precious Children Home and 284 children have graduated now. He rewrote the earlier concept of missions. In a time when mission work was considered a career served by professionals, Dr. Allen showed the Virginia Baptist the concept of volunteer missions. Not only he showed through his life, he attracted several pastors of Virginia and beyond and showed them the why and how of volunteer missions and got them involved.

Ray has condensed his biography or else this would have been pages and pages, so extensive is his life and accomplishments.

Behind the success of Ray, there is Ann, his wife. Ray is blessed with a son and two daughters and five grand children. They are all my friends.

I am privileged to write an introduction to this book where Dr. Ray Allen unfolds the secrets of how to be a Christian happy and successful. The opportunities I had to work with him in India and the U.S., the encouragements I received from him, the way he equipped and mentored me are his investments in my life. I thank Ray for giving me this honor. May the good Lord bless the readers. With these words let me introduce this book to readers and surrender it at the feet of Jesus, the Carpenter of Nazareth who Ray claims as his boss and I join Ray in that claim.

AUTHOR'S PREFACE

I was sitting in a laundry mat in Maneo, North Carolina, watching my family's clothes dry. A carnival was in town and a boy from the carnival approached me.

"Mister, what racket are you in?"

My reply, "I am the pastor of a Baptist church."

His response, "Oh, you have a big tent and take up lots of money."

Smiling, I said, "No."

Frowning he said, "Oh, you are on T.V. and get lots of money."

I had no luck getting him to understand. Probably many people are as confused as he was about who a pastor is and what he or she does.

Perhaps it is a racket, as part of the job is talking those who have into supporting, witnessing, and sharing with those who do not.

Many have encouraged me to tell my story. At the young age of 75, I decided to give it a try if for no other reason than for my children and grandchildren to perhaps understand me better.

Every part of this has been a struggle—even what to call the story was not easy. Consideration was given to *The Road from Burley Hollow*, the small hollow in rural Amherst County, Virginia where I spent my teen years; and to *Taj Mahal*, which

I have visited many times. Then perhaps *From White Trash to Trailer Trash* because when I grew up, sometimes the town kids called me white trash to my face. I also remember as a child that when I fed the jailer's cows, his wife made me come to the back door of their residence to be paid. When we decided to retire, we bought a travel trailer and roamed the U.S and Canada for 15 months. Our grandson told his Sunday school class that his grandparents had moved into a trailer. Some in the church became concerned that we had fallen on hard times. We were fine—we had just decided to spend winters in the Crooked Hook RV Resort, Clewiston, Florida. *My Racket* became the obvious choice.

I was born on April 13, 1938, in the village of Lowesville, Virginia. A little less than a year later, my father, Raymond Smith Allen, died in lumber camp a few miles up the Little Piney River from the village. A year later my mother married his younger brother who soon became an alcoholic. Most autobiographical reflections would start there. I do not plan to share much of my unhappy childhood because as I remember it, I was the unloved stepchild. Later I will share some of the childhood experiences that affected my life.

The most important event of my life happened shortly after I got my driver's permit at 15. I had my first date with a 5-foot, 100-pound classmate, Ann Cobb. We dated all through high school. For the first time in my life, it became clear to me that not only did I love her, but she loved me. She was the first person I ever knew who loved me and saw potential in me. So as not to hold the reader in suspense, we married on July 13, 1957, three months after my nineteenth birthday, and we're still married. Her love transformed my life.

In high school few of the teachers encouraged me. They rightly believed that I would stay in my hollow and cut pulpwood. They also believed that when Ann went to college, she would find a more suitable husband.

One of my teachers was different—John D. Smith, my chemistry teacher. He believed I could go to college. He took me to see Virginia Tech and explained its program of allowing me to study engineering for one quarter, after which Tech would find me a job for the second quarter. I worked long hours at a sawmill, saved almost every penny I made, bought one used uniform, and spent the fall of 1955 at Virginia Tech. That fall, the university changed the program so that a student had to stay in school for two quarters before they would place him in a job. I only had one nickel at the end of the quarter. I hitchhiked home and was back at the sawmill the next day. No bank would loan me the $300 to continue. I borrowed a car, returned to Blacksburg, and dropped out of school. As I drove, at perhaps the lowest point in my life, I resolved to forget this place of disappointment and never return.

THE LONGEST DAY

On a cold January 16, 1956, I caught a very early bus to Roanoke, Virginia, to be inducted into the Army. As I rode, I was tremendously happy to be escaping from poverty, the memories of emotional and physical abuse, and the embarrassment of not being able to continue at Tech. Deep down I was also scared to death. Perhaps this would be another lost dream. Everywhere I had been thus far, this poor boy from a mountain hollow found the world was stacked against him. It appeared for a while even the army was not going to take me. Due to the stress I was under, I had to rest in a dark room to get my blood pressure down to an acceptable level. As soon as that happened—5 o'clock that afternoon—I was sworn into the U. S. Army.

There were five of us new recruits. They loaded us into an airport limo and drove us to Fort Jackson, South Carolina. As I rode in the first limo I had ever been in, I thought, "This is great—soon we'll be sleeping in a barracks." Arriving at the post just past midnight, we were surprised to be issued our uniforms and all of our equipment. At 0300 hours they divided us into squads, took us to tents, and told us to put our gear neatly away.

When we finished making our beds, the corporal told us to get some sleep because tomorrow we'd be taking all of the tests to see what we would do in the army. Very timidly I asked, "Sir, what time do we get up?" He replied, "Soldier, I am not a damn officer in this army. Only officers are addressed as 'Sir'. You will refer to me as Corporal. If you ever refer to me or any noncom as 'Sir', you will give me 50 pushups. Is that clear? I will wake you up at 0430. You will make your bunk, clean your area, and police up the area around the tent. When you hear my whistle at 0500, you will have your sorry ass at attention in the breakfast formation. Lights out! Hit the sack!"

I sat down on my bunk, held my tired head in my hands, and asked myself, what have I done? Stepped out of the frying pan into the fire? Little did I know that this was the first day of my new, exciting life.

BASIC TRAINING

True to his word, at 0430 the corporal returned banging two trash can lids together and screaming, "Off your sorry ass and on your feet!" After he had checked our bunks and the tent for orderliness and cleanliness, he marched us to a large mess hall. We put the food on metal trays and sat down to eat. The corporal stalked between the tables barking, "Swallow it! We don't have all day!" Immediately after choking down our chow, we were marched to a large classroom and tested on everything imaginable.

After lunch he marched us back to our tents. We had no instructions in marching yet every few minutes he stopped the march to single someone out for not knowing how to march. He could have written dirty novels because he used words to describe our mothers and our sexual identities that neither I nor my fellow workers at the sawmill had ever heard before. Back at the tents, we were told to put all of our belongings in our duffel bags and get ready to move out. Trucks arrived and we loaded everything on to them. We then marched to the barber shop to have our hair shaved off. As each recruit left the barber shop, he was loaded on to a truck with no explanation of what was coming next.

Soon we arrived at C Company 502, Regiment 101, Airborne Division. Sergeant First Class Scotto greeted us with little excitement. He wore the famous screaming eagle patch as well as emblems of several WWII battles. He informed us that we were so fortunate that our training was going to be given by the meanest, toughest soldiers in the army. He further explained that the 101st had won World War II with little help from the rest of the army. He assured us that he was the toughest of the tough and if anybody doubted that to step forward and he would prove it. The heavyweight champion of Puerto Rico was in the group, but he did not dare accept the sergeant's challenge. He explained his job was to turn us into a tough fighting machine. He said the army would be what we made of it. We could get along by doing what he told us, or he would make it so hard on us that we would wish we had never been born.

After his introductory speech, he divided us into platoons and assigned each platoon a barracks. I was placed in the first platoon. We were dismissed and told to put our gear away and be ready when the whistle blew for mess formation. At formation, several names were called out including mine, and we were told to report to the day room at 1900 hours for a meeting with the company commander.

Everyone whose name had been called arrived at the day room 10 minutes early. It was a mixture of draftees, volunteers, and several reservists or National Guard members doing their six months' active duty. No one had any idea what to expect. There were three or four National Guard sergeants in the group. Capt. Williams, the company commander, arrived. We all came to attention and saluted. He welcomed us to the company and introduced us to the company clerk, Specialist Carter. Capt. Williams explained that all of our training would be under Sergeant Scotto's guidance and that of his assistants, Corporal Wells and Private First Class Kelley.

Then he said, "Our records indicate that all of you have completed at least one unit of R.O.T.C. If you have not, you can return to the barracks. Specialist Carter, divide these people into four groups and you and the cadre carry on."

The specialist separated the reserve sergeants from the rest of us. Then he divided those who had been part of a cadet corps into a separate group. Then Sergeant Scotto took over. He divided us into groups of six: a reservist sergeant, a former cadet corps member, and four former ROTC students. I am sure at 17 years old; I was the youngest person in the room.

He came to our group first. Without any hesitation, he said, "Sergeant Foster, you will be the platoon sergeant of the first platoon. Allen, you will be the student assistant platoon sergeant. Here are your acting—very temporary—sergeant stripes. Your job is to do what Sergeant Foster tells you to do. The rest of you will be squad leaders. Here are your temporary corporal stripes. Now go get your platoon organized."

Sergeant Foster stopped at the entrance of the barracks, turned and said, "Two of the squad leaders need to be downstairs, two up. Since I am downstairs, Allen needs to be up. Each of you squad leaders, take one side of the barracks. Each of you pick a man and report to Sergeant Allen right after breakfast to clean the latrine. Let's get organized, men. I am going to bed—Sergeant Allen will answer your questions."

At 0500 the Charge of Quarters (the noncommissioned officer who is responsible for the company at night or on holidays) came through the barracks blowing a whistle and barking, "Off your ass and on your feet! Get your bunks made! Clean your area! The latrine better be clean enough for the old man (company commander) to eat his breakfast off the floor! Inspection is at 0550." Quickly, I got my area ready then asked the squad leaders for the soldiers who had latrine duty. I assigned one of the squad leaders to oversee the latrine cleaning. I set out to check each soldier's area. Sergeant Scotto found only small things wrong, but he took delight in chewing the soldiers out. He told us when we heard the whistle to fall out for breakfast.

Breakfast formation revealed that we had a clinger and other goof-offs in our platoon. It was our job to straighten them out because we would be punished until we did. One soldier stepped to the front and urinated in front of all of us. Another walked leisurely to formation several minutes late. Our punishment: we ate last. The formation for lunch was a reenactment of breakfast. The clinger proceeded to relieve himself in front of everyone again. Sergeant Scotto told him, "You can do anything you want, but you are in the army to stay." Our tardy soldier was tardy again. Our punishment was again to be the last group to eat. At the supper formation things changed. Two soldiers grabbed our tardy soldier by the arms; two others took socks with a bar of soap in them and beat him in the behind as the first two dragged him down the stairs to the formation. He complained to Sergeant Scotto, who asked for witnesses. No one had seen anything. The sergeant told him to get his slow ass back in ranks, and that he better be sure when he heard the whistle, he beat everyone else down the steps. At the breakfast formation, before the whistle blew, that soldier was standing in the ranks at attention. We never ate last again.

At 17 the youngest person in the platoon, I knew my leadership would be challenged. It happened in week two. Most of the soldiers in our platoon were draftees. That meant they were in their 20s and not happy to be in the army. A 6 foot 6 inch 250-pound draftee from the streets of Philadelphia made the challenge. He was on latrine duty. I told him to re-mop the floor. He replied, "If you didn't have those stripes, you wouldn't tell me to do anything." I removed my temporary stripes, looked him square in the eyes, and said, "They're off. Let's go behind the barracks."

He was 70 pounds heavier and 4 inches taller. I was nervous, but not afraid. In elementary school I had attended eight different schools and one of them three separate times. The first day at a new school, I had always had to fight the class bully. In the fourth grade I decided I was tired of being beaten up. So I learned to fight. In the sixth grade we moved to Covington, Virginia. At the first recess Leon challenged me to a fight. I knocked two of his permanent teeth out. The principal came, heard what happened, and said, "Looks like Leon got what he had coming to him. You boys better become friends with the new boy." My experience taught me when challenged, get the first lick in, and make it a good one.

With this in mind, I brought my knee up into the private's groin full force. When he bent over in pain, I knocked him down and put my knee in his chest. Adding insult to injury, I slapped him several times across the face. He was crying, saying, "You don't fight fair, but I'll mop the latrine if you'll let me up." Then I saw that the whole platoon had gathered to watch. Sergeant Scotto commented, "Men, in war, if you fight fair, you get killed. Let this be a lesson that you always fight to win. And you always shoot first."

There were no more serious challenges to my leadership. Basic training was not difficult because I had carried a 70-pound chainsaw up and down the mountainside since I was fourteen years old. We marched and went through extensive physical training every day. Captain Summers, a hero of the Battle of the Bulge, taught us to throw grenades. We learned hand-to-hand combat and how to fight during a gas attack.

I soon learned that if the training was to be done in the South Carolina sand or heavy rain, Sergeant Foster was going to have a reason to stay in the barracks and I was to lead the platoon. The day we crawled the obstacle course was one of the days he had important things to do in the company. In this course the soldiers started in a deep ditch and crawled around mine fields which exploded if anyone got too close. On the first try, no one had any problems. On the second try, they added machine gun fire 18 inches above our heads. The instructor had a steel helmet which had bullet holes going through it. He claimed that a soldier had stood up when he crawled onto a snake on the course. Supposedly he died on the scene. Later we crawled the course at night. Everyone was scared to say the least, but no one in the first platoon panicked. We all made it through.

Since Sergeant Foster had qualified with firearms at his guard unit, he did not have to go to the rifle range. We marched the 10 miles to the range with a full pack and rifle. Each of us had half a shelter, so we had to pair up to have a dry place to sleep. Sergeant Scotto told the platoon sergeants to have the soldiers pitch their tents, dig a prone fox hole, and be ready for tank training the next day. When I checked the troops, two of our Puerto Rican soldiers had understood the sergeant to say, "Tomorrow, we will drive tanks over you." So they had dug foxholes six feet deep. Throughout basic training, bells of learning were going off in my head. This taught me that a leader always needs to be sure everyone understands what they need to do.

Throughout basic training, we were told repeatedly that we were always to look after our fellow soldiers and that the 101st never leaves a fellow soldier behind. In most of the training exercises, we were required to work in teams of two. On the rifle range your buddy coached you and you coached him.

One evening one of the sergeants called a meeting of the platoon sergeants and said he wanted to see the goof-offs in each of the platoons digging six by six holes behind the barracks. I saw no value in this sort of unwarranted punishment. Nevertheless, it was an order. I picked the lowest-performing soldier in the platoon and had him start digging. I checked on him. In the dark I could hear crying and two voices cursing me. At first it made me angry. But when I walked over, I found his buddy from the rifle range was in the hole helping him dig. Then it occurred to me—we were becoming a band of brothers, and those two guys had learned enough. I told them to cover the hole up and go get a good night's sleep.

After ten weeks, basic training was over. Before enlisting I had taken a mechanics test and been guaranteed that I would go to helicopter mechanic's school. When the orders came down, I was assigned for training with the Air Force. The company commander called me into his office and said his noncommissioned officers had been watching me. He asked me to stay and be a part of the training cadre, but the choice was mine. If I chose to stay, he would promote me to corporal as soon as I finished advanced infantry training. I thanked him, but decided to go on to helicopter school in Texas.

REFLECTIONS ON BASIC TRAINING

As I rode home on leave, I knew the insecure 17-year-old who saw himself as a loser, destined to find the world stacked against him, was not me anymore. Instead, I was going home confident that at least in the army, it didn't matter who your parents were, where you grew up or how old you were. They would give you a chance. I was proud to step off the bus in my uniform. When I did, the owner of the Greek restaurant in Amherst came out of the restaurant, shook my hand, thanked me for my service to this wonderful country, gave me a Coke and said, "It would be a privilege for me to have you eat any meal you want while you are at my restaurant. It's on the house." His kindness still brings tears to my eyes.

The army had given me the opportunity to lead, and being a leader was better than being a follower. Most of the leaders I had known spent a great deal of effort making sure that those under them did not become leaders. The great secret of the army was that a leader cared for those he led, taught them their jobs by example, and disciplined them when they missed the mark but encouraged them and rewarded them when they succeeded. From those days to this, the idea of a leader has been and always will be the example set by my junior noncommissioned officers in the military.

For the first time in my life, there was a little money in my pocket. I could buy a Pepsi if I wanted it. Indeed, I was often very reckless with money. Many evenings I went to the PX, bought a pint of ice cream and ate it on the steps of the barracks. I had been taught that the poor were blessed (Jesus said poor in spirit). I remember wondering at the time who made that up. I was sure it was some rich lord. I soon realized it was definitely better to have some money in your pocket.

Living with people from all over the country also challenged many things my culture had taught me. Southern Virginia was a hotbed of racism in the 1950s. In the army I lived with African-Americans, and had African-American officers and NCO's. I was going home understanding that they wanted the same things I wanted—a better future for themselves and their families.

Many of my religious beliefs were being challenged as well. I saw ladies at the PX who were military wives who smoked, and I was sure they weren't street walkers. I met Roman Catholics who were devout and good and decent. I observed that Episcopalians could hold their beer a lot better than my Baptist brothers. In fact, there was at least one atheist who was a caring person. Often my understanding of passages of Scripture just did not stand up to reason. I was not at all sure that I would continue in my Christian faith. However, I did go to church on leave, primarily because Rev. L.L. Schweimer, my pastor, and Jenny Lee Massie, my Sunday school teacher, were two of the most caring people I had ever known.

The ten weeks of basic training had planted the seeds of positive change in my life. My journey of learning and change was just beginning. If you read to the end, you will see how it all worked out some 57 years later.

GARY AIR FORCE BASE, SAN MARCOS, TEXAS

On April 7, 1956, at 9:00 p.m., I boarded a commercial airliner for Washington, D.C. with a final destination of Austin, Texas. At 10:00 the next morning, we landed in Austin. Since it was early spring in Virginia, I had to wear my winter uniform which was very heavy and 100% wool. The temperature in Austin was in the high 90s. I thought I would roast. Two soldiers and I took an unairconditioned cab to the base.

Two days later at 6:00 a.m., classes began. Due to the heat and no air conditioning, we were through at 2:00 in the afternoon. The instructors were either Air Force NCO's or civilians. Military training is the best I've ever experienced. First they lectured on all aspects of the H-13, the small helicopter everyone has seen on "MASH". Then you immediately went to a helicopter and performed the procedure you had been taught. Each test was written and you performed a repair while being observed by an instructor. In ten weeks you were a fully-trained mechanic. Later—either on the job or in a two week course—you transitioned to the larger cargo helicopters.

My days were spent in class. As soon as class was over, most of us would go to the swimming pool for a couple of hours. In the evening we studied. Since every graduate except those in the Reserve or National Guard were sent to Korea, we assumed we would all be sent there when we graduated.

About midway through the training school a life-changing event occurred. I was walking back to class from lunch. I saw a long line going into the school's administration building. One of the instructors spoke to me and told me the army was going to open its own aviation school at Fort Rucker, Alabama, and that a group of civilians and officers were here interviewing people to be instructors. He told me to get in line. I asked, "Why?" He replied, "Don't you know you are the number one student in your class?" I had never been first in anything in my life. I got into the line, was interviewed, and expected nothing to come of it. After all, they still sent every graduate to Korea.

In August my class graduated. After the brief graduation ceremony, our orders were read. Having a last name beginning with A, my name was always near the top of the list. They read the names of the entire class, except mine. They all received leave and orders to report to Fort Lewis, Washington, and proceed to Korea. Then my name was read to report to the Headquarters Company, The Army Aviation School, Fort Rucker, Alabama. We were dismissed and told we could leave immediately.

Meanwhile things were not going well at home. My stepfather had developed a serious cancer. Midway through school, the Red Cross had obtained for me an emergency leave and loaned me the money to go home. He was still critically ill. Since I only had travel money to go from Texas to Alabama, I decided to ride the train home.

At the station I sent Ann a telegram stating, "I am going to Fort Rucker to teach. I love you." The telegraph operator smiled and said, "Young man, you think the first sentence of your message is important, but if you marry that young lady, the last will be more important. Never forget to say it over and over."

I spent most of my ten-day leave visiting my stepfather in the veterans' hospital and helping my mother. I gave her most of the small amount of money I had. Then I caught a bus for the 24-hour ride to Fort Rucker, Alabama.

Most importantly, I gave Ann an engagement ring. Neither family seemed very happy—her family because she was planning to marry someone below their social standing—my family because I was marrying above my raising. They were both right.

FT. RUCKER

I arrived at Fort Rucker excited but anxious. Throughout my teen years, I had acute stage fright. In high school I had taken an F rather than recite a poem I still know before the class. When I reported to the company, the company commander informed me that I would begin instructor's school on Monday. If I passed as a Category One Instructor, then I would be assigned to teach both mechanics and the ground school for the flight school. If I passed as a Category Two Instructor, then I would be allowed to teach under a qualified instructor until he decided I could handle a class. If I failed, I would probably be transferred to another post. In my mind that meant Korea.

Instructors' school started at 6:30 a.m. In the class were several privates along with several warrant officers and commissioned officers including one major. All of the officers were pilots.

The army must have recognized stage fright as a major problem. The class began with the instructor calling a student by name and telling him to tell the story of his life in five minutes. He began with the officers. The major began his talk with, "In 1938 I entered the army." I was next and said, "The year the major entered the army I was born." The class roared with laughter. I relaxed and shared my story. Throughout the class the instructors worked on helping us overcome our stage fright. Some days on the desk there would be pieces of paper with a topic written on them. When you were called, you walked up, picked up a piece of paper, and gave a five minute lecture on the subject. My topic was, *Should Prostitution Be Legalized?*

On other days each of us gave a five minute lecture on a subject we felt we knew well. My topic was on the ways to skin a squirrel. Some days each of us led a 15 minute class on some aspect of aircraft repair. For the final exam, we each taught a one-hour class. Each hour of instruction was to have an introduction that caught the students' attention. After the attention-getter, we were to tell the student why he needed to know the subject. Then we were to tell him what he needed to know, and then tell him again. Our finish was to be a closing statement that the soldier would never forget. To this day this is the outline I follow every time I make a speech.

The commander of the school, a full bird colonel, spoke at our graduation. I had wondered how the army would handle a buck private teaching officers. The colonel made it clear. He said, "This is a unique time in aviation. You are the first instructors in our school. You will write the lesson plans, teach the classes, and give the tests. Whatever grade you give, will stand. It will not be changed. Every student will be told that, and further, you are in charge of that classroom. When you teach, you teach representing me. Teach every mechanic and every pilot so that you would be comfortable riding the helicopter they repair or fly. My diploma read, "Category One Instructor" and my military specialty was changed to "Senior Aviation Instructor."

My first class was at 6:30 a.m. Monday after graduation on Friday. In my department was Lt. Holey, a warrant officer, a civilian instructor, and another private. I arrived early, put my notes on the podium, the lesson plan on a desk in the back reserved for the Inspector Instructors and went to the bathroom. Even though the time in instructors' school largely dealt with my stage fright problem, I was still nervous. As I stepped on the platform, the class came to attention; the class leader saluted, and reported the class was all in attendance. When I looked down, my notes were gone. Lt. Holey was sitting at the inspector's desk with a big smile on his face. I had to teach the class without a single note.

At the end of the hour, I respectfully asked the lieutenant why he did that. He responded, "Allen, I know you know the subject; now you know you know the subject."

It was an exciting time to teach in the Aviation School. We were training fixed wing pilots who were usually lieutenants or captains to be helicopter pilots. There were enlisted men going to helicopter school who graduated as warrant officers and helicopter pilots. Both of these groups took the same classes as the mechanics, but they did not do the practical exercises. We could turn out a first class mechanic in 90 days. The students worked hard because aviation companies were excellent places to serve. Each day we worked on lesson plans and taught our classes. Often we went out to the Aviation Board located at Fort Rucker where the army tested future aircraft.

Each instructor in our department developed areas of expertise. I loved and taught most of the engine troubleshooting. We had engines with controls that the students could run up to and diagnose the problem. We spent hours dreaming up ways to create engine problems—cigarette filters in ignition leads to the spark plugs to make them misfire; thin wires in magneto points; and restrictions in air filters or gas lines to create misfires. Every student in all three courses had to pass a troubleshooting test before he could leave our department. Later they may well have to evaluate the problem in flight which could cause or prevent a crash.

Even in training, army activities are dangerous. Flying helicopters and landing on tank roads is very different than a Sunday drive in the country. Making the transition from flying a fixed wing aircraft to rotary wing helicopters is difficult. The first of my students to crash and die was a lieutenant who was an excellent fixed wing pilot. He took off on a cool fall morning and the carburetor iced up. In a fixed wing, the pilot pulled the carburetor heat with the right hand. In a helicopter, the pilot reaches across with the left hand and pulls the carburetor heat. The lieutenant released the control stick and pulled with his right hand. He lost control and went in from about a thousand feet. Death was instant. He left a wife and two children.

Nevertheless, I wanted very badly to go to helicopter flight school and fly. I inquired and learned I could teach in the school at eighteen years old, but I had to be 20 and a half to attend it. Such are the rules and ways of the army. Later they took away the age requirement, and some of the pilots in Vietnam were 19-year-olds.

In November, the civilian mechanics at the Rucker airport went on strike. The post commander decided that the pilots' training needed to continue and that this would also discourage the strikers if everything continued without them. The instructors would be the crew chiefs and the advance students would be the crew. We were to work beginning at six in the evening and quit when we were finished. The students and I were assigned 12 helicopters. Most of the work was normal maintenance much like a service station. We filled them up with gas, checked the oil, and corrected any problems the pilot put in the flight log. The students did the work, and I checked their work and signed the log. We had no problems except the cold and sleeping in an army barracks in the day time. It would get down in the thirties after dark with the humidity percentage in the 90's. The dampness would cut you to the bone. You could not wear gloves and do the work. The aircraft felt like an icebox. After ten days the mechanics came back to work. It was excellent training for the students, but everyone was glad when it was over.

As soon as I was eligible, I was promoted to private first class. Things could not have been going better. I enjoyed teaching and loved army aviation. I began to think about marrying Ann and bringing her to Alabama. The only problem with my dreams was that my stepfather's health continued to decline. I was trying to get by on less than twenty dollars per month. The Red Cross was letting me pay back the loan I had taken for my emergency leave while in helicopter school at a dollar a week. The rest was going home to help support my mother and nine half-brothers and sisters.

Lieutenant Holey in my department learned from the Red Cross of my difficulty. He advised me to get a compassion discharge. I told him I wanted to stay in the army and become a pilot. He then suggested a transfer to the transportation school at Fort Eustis, Virginia. He and the Red Cross soon had my transfer approved. The Red Cross sent me a letter saying my debt was forgiven and wished me success in the future. With deep gratitude I resolved if I could ever do anything for the Red Cross, I would. In mid-December with deep sadness, I caught a bus for Fort Eustis.

It seemed at the time that nothing good happening to me would ever last. Yet I knew for the first time, there are people who really care and will help others.

FORT EUSTIS

Unfortunately, when my orders were cut at Fort Rucker, they were not to report to the transportation school, but to report to Fort Eustis. This meant that I went to a receiving and processing company. This also meant that those in personnel decided where I was most needed on the post. After being there for only a few days, my stepfather died. I was given a ten day emergency leave which lasted past Christmas.

His death was truly a tragedy. In retrospect, I realized he obviously had severe mood swings. As is often the case with alcoholics, he could be devotedly religious or hostile toward religion. He always had a quick, violent temper. Riding the bus home, my feelings were split. Prior to leaving for the army, I had asked him to consider returning to church and getting his life straight. He laughed at me and said the next time he went to church; it would be in a casket. His prediction was now true. Right or wrong, I have never shed the first tear for him. The physical and emotional abuse from my relationship with him still affects me in low moments of my life. I knew his death would complicate it even more. This was before the many programs that we now have for the poor. He had left my mother and nine children from one year old to 16 year old living in a rented house with no income. I knew I would have to help even more. We buried him beside my father; I helped his brothers cover his grave.

When I returned to the base, I went to the finance office and applied for a dependent allowance for three of my half siblings. Fortunately, it was quickly approved and with what I added, they received approximately $200 monthly, and I received less than $50 to live on. My half-sister, Roxie Ann, worked 20 hours a week at a department store and gave most of her pay to the family. She was very bright and had excellent grades. The situation, however, made it impossible for her to consider going to college.

The army and my difficulties in life were making me very good at suppressing my feelings, hunkering down, and doing what I had to do. The lines from the Doris Day song of the time "Whatever will be, will be; the future is not mine you see," spoke volumes to me. I knew damn well I had no control over the future. The next event confirmed my view.

A few days after returning from emergency leave, I went to post personnel to be assigned to my new duties. A sergeant reviewed my records without asking me a single question. He told me that the 582nd Transportation Company was being brought up to strength, and he had been ordered to assign all aviation mechanics to that unit. He handed me my written orders and told me to report immediately to Capt. Graves, the company commander. As I took the orders, he asked, "What does the last number in your military specialty mean?" I replied, "Senior Aviation Instructor." He remarked, "Probably you should be sent to the transportation school, but it is too much trouble to redo the orders."

I reported to the captain. He said that they were one of two heavy maintenance companies in the army. The other was stationed in Germany. The task of the company was to repair the aircraft of the 101st Airborne Infantry which was being turned into a helicopter assault regiment. He said we also had to be up to date with our weapons and training so that we could go anywhere in the world in 72 hours. He reviewed my records and said, "I am sorry you cannot be a part of the 582nd because you got a compassionate transfer, and we are leaving for 90 days maneuvers in February." I told him my reason for the transfer had died and if I had a choice, I would rather stay. I was getting a very positive feeling about the captain. He was a World War II veteran and a senior army aviator. He asked me about my schooling and experience and shared that there were no experienced NCO's to be crew chiefs and if I could handle the job, he would like for me to be a crew chief. I readily agreed to do my best.

The 582nd consisted of a rotary wing platoon, a fixed wing platoon and a shop platoon. I was part of the rotary wing platoon. The platoon sergeant was Sergeant First Class Smith who did have experience in aviation. There was a Specialist Three who was the technical inspector for all aircraft. He had civilian experience in aviation and had been in the army a couple of years. There was another specialist who had been in the service for two or three years but had little experience in aviation. The company had two pilots; one was a first lieutenant, the other a second lieutenant. There was a warrant officer who was a maintenance warrant, and another who was a specialist in parts and supply. Most of the personnel were privates or privates first class just out of school. Every one of them was an excellent mechanic.

Most of January was spent getting tools together and getting trucks ready to haul our equipment to Fort Polk, Louisiana for maneuvers. We had trucks to haul the equipment required to accomplish our mission. Each enlisted man had a driver's license for all of the vehicles assigned to him. The crew chiefs all had "run up and taxi" licenses for the aircraft they were to work on. On the first Monday in February, 1956, we hit the road in convoy for the five day trip to Fort Polk. I drove a ¾ quarter ton Dodge all terrain pickup. I did not have a second driver, but one of the pilots rode with me. Since all of the vehicles were tactical vehicles, we sounded like a train going down the road.

On day three on the road, a World War II veteran had an attack of malaria and became very ill. Captain Graves sent his driver for me. He told me to drive the soldier to a hospital in Atlanta, Georgia. He said he was sending Lt. Bailey with me because an officer had to sign the papers to admit the solder to the hospital. Then he told me that under no circumstances was I to let Lt. Herman drive the truck because he did not have a truck driver's license. This put me in a difficult position. When the lieutenant asked me to drive, I certainly did not want him upset with me. As politely as I could, I told him that the captain had ordered me to do all of the driving. I drove right down Peachtree Street with many people staring at us because they had never seen an army off road vehicle. The soldier's health improved and he returned to duty in a couple of weeks. Late that night we arrived at the air force base where we were staying.

After five days on the road, we arrived at Fort Polk, Louisiana. The soldiers playing the war games in the maneuvers were staying in tents. We were assigned to barracks. We arrived in the evening. In a company meeting, the first sergeant told us we would have Saturday and Sunday to write home and put our gear away. He said our Class A passes were good here just as they were at Eustis, and we could go into town but beware of the women—some would be looking for husbands. Also, we needed to be ready to work very hard and long hours and he had better not see anyone hung over.

Monday morning we went to the Fort Polk airfield and set up our maintenance tents. These tents were large enough to bring a helicopter inside. We soon found it was cooler to work outside in the sun. After everything was squared away, Maintenance Sergeant Carter had a meeting to explain to us our role which would be much like an automobile dealer. The crew chief flying with the helicopter daily would do the routine service and maintenance. The major repairs and inspections would be our job. Whenever we received an aircraft, one of our crew chiefs would make a total list of needed repairs and inspections. Then the crew chief would assign at least two mechanics to do the repairs. After a test flight with one of our pilots, the crew chief, the tech inspector, and the pilot would sign off and notify the unit to retrieve their aircraft. Most parts would be available in the parts tent. If they were not, there was an aircraft available to fly to the St. Louis Army Depot and bring the needed parts back. This meant that sometimes the plane was sent to St. Louis for a part that was available in town for a couple of dollars. We were to return the aircraft to duty as soon as possible. The crew chief could not have a day off until the aircraft was ready to fly.

The helicopter platoon was divided into four crews of approximately ten men each. Specialist Daniels and I were the crew chiefs for the reconnaissance helicopters. These are the helicopters seen on the television show "MASH." Many of them were used to spot targets and ferry the brass around to observe war games.

We were very busy with interesting and challenging work. Lt. Davis was our chief test pilot and flew most of the test flights. He was always supportive of the crews and frequently asked about their work. Flying with him was like flying with eagles. During our stay, he brought several helicopters down with complete engine failure. One day we watched him take off and heard the engine fail at less than 500 hundred feet. Every person stopped his work saw him go down in thick pine trees. We all began running toward where we expected to find him dead. Instead, when we got there he was standing in a tank road looking at the engine. There was water in the gasoline which had caused the failure. The crew chief drained the tank and refilled it. He and Lt. Toner took off and completed the test flight. I flew with him the next day on a test flight. I commented that it took a lot of guts to complete the test flight. He laughed and said, "I had to if I was ever going to fly again."

The army often sent in brass from the Pentagon to have us test the use of helicopters for new duties. While at Fort Polk, they decided to use an H34 cargo helicopter to recover crashed helicopters. They sent a hotshot pilot who had gained his reputation flying brass around and used our recovery crew. With the cameras rolling, their pilot came in, flared out, and dropped the crashed helicopter from 20 feet in the air. Our Test pilot volunteered to take our crew and do it the next day. To the surprise of the assembled brass, he set the crashed helicopter down like it was a featherbed.

We fixed everything with only one unpleasant incident. Daniels had done a great deal of work on a helicopter. On the day he was to finish the job, he became ill. My crew completed the repairs and the test flight. I was unaware that the regular crew chief and Daniels had had some strong words. Daniels had forbidden the crew chief from talking to his men. Shortly after the regular pilot took the helicopter back to the unit, he returned in a jeep. He accused me of removing a bolt from the flight controls and trying to kill him. He gave me what is called in the army a first class ass-chewing. Captain Loveland came out and began chewing out the pilot saying, "If you have problems with our work, you come to me, and I will chew out my own men." They checked the records and neither Daniels nor I had worked on the flight controls. Later that day, one of the unit's sergeants checked their mechanics' tool box and found the bolt which the mechanic had removed in an effort to get even with Daniels. Captain Davis, in defending me, grew in everyone's respect.

In May, 1957 we returned to Fort Eustis. The first weekend we were back the entire company was given a three-day pass. All those who lived close by or could afford to fly went home for the three days. We spent the month of May cleaning our equipment and putting it away.

Shortly after returning, I was promoted to Specialist Three. At the time, the army only had seven enlisted ranks. It also meant that I had reached the middle rate fairly rapidly, but it also meant that in a peacetime army that was as far as I could go. This was a nice increase in pay. I decided that I would not tell my family about my pay increase. Instead, I told them that soon I would have to stop sending any of my pay homes, and they would only receive what the army was paying for the children I had claimed as dependents. I also bought my first car—a 1952 Dodge—on credit.

Ann and I had been discussing getting married. The truth was I did not have any money at all at the end of the month. Nevertheless, we decided to get married and keep it a secret. On July 13th, two of our childhood friends went with us to get married in Cumberland, Virginia. We had no money to do anything special and knew both of our mothers would be upset. I borrowed the money from Ann to buy gas to return to the base. She continued to work at her summer job and went back to college in the fall. The first day I was back at work I added her to my army records, making her the beneficiary of my G.I. insurance. This meant her allowance as a wife was also an increase in salary. I had the money sent to me and saved it for the day she could come and join me at Fort Eustis. This was not the best way to begin a marriage—two teenagers from totally different backgrounds with no family support and very little money.

During the rest of the summer, the company was put on light duty which meant we trained or worked on aircraft for a half day. The biggest problem an army has in peacetime is boredom. We spent a week at the rifle range. I had to qualify on the carbine and .45 caliber pistol. The company commander made me the hand-to-hand combat instructor. It became one of my jobs to be sure all of the company knew how to kill with a bayonet and their bare hands. All of the crew chiefs were also sent to factory schools, so they would be qualified on all of the aircraft the army used.

On the other half day, we were involved in sports. The rivalry between units in the army depicted on "MASH" is realistic. During that time, six of us were the 582nd Transportation Company's volleyball team. For a month we practiced and competed against other companies' teams, winning the post championship and receiving a three-day pass for our efforts. In the fall we did various jobs, sometimes repairing aircraft at the airport or at the transportation school.

We also put on demonstrations for the brass. The army was trying to sell the Pentagon on the concept of using helicopters in combat. The local leaders were clearly afraid to use the infantry to demonstrate, so everyone involved was a fully-trained helicopter mechanic accustomed to working around whirling helicopter blades. Sometimes we hit the beach from a landing craft. Our rifles would be blazing as we made a quick assault in front of the grandstands. A "flying banana" would come in and pick us up. In other exercises, we would be brought in by helicopter to make our quick raid, then taken out by helicopter in just a few minutes. The army was successful in developing the new role for helicopters in combat. Some of the things we did are still used in combat today.

At Christmas that year Ann and I decided we had to tell our parents and set up housekeeping. In January we told her mother. She was naturally disappointed but pleaded with us for Ann to finish school. At the time my feelings were hurt, but now, as a parent myself, I understand her disappointment. We assured her Ann would finish school. (After having helped put me through a doctoral degree and having three children, she graduated from Radford University one quarter after our oldest daughter graduated.) My mother warned me I had married above my raising and would regret it. I never have.

Ann finished her quarter at Radford and her mother gave us a reception to announce our marriage. We rented a two-room apartment in Williamsburg, Virginia and began our life together. In many ways we were two wounded people. Ann's father had died from cancer when she was seven. He was away most of the time because he was an engineer on the Pan-American Highway and at several naval bases in Trinidad. She had been raised by her grandmother (Mama Sallie), who was a caring and good human being. Ann's mother, Kate Cobb, had been left with medical bills and a small social security check to raise a daughter. Kate made her way to the top when women were supposed to be secretaries or stay at home. She retired as the manager of the Lynchburg Employment Office having turned down frequent opportunities to be promoted and transferred to the central office in Richmond. Because of the deaths of both our fathers, neither Ann nor I had any role models for what a good marriage was like.

My assistant crew chief, Darwin Modlin, and one of my crew members, Hosea Garica, each got married at nearly the same time I did. So we became friends as couples. Since all of us had little money, we entertained ourselves by having picnics and going to the 25-cent movies on post. Soon it was obvious that all three women in our group were pregnant. Our daughter, Ann Elizabeth Allen (Beth), was born in the Fort Eustis Army Hospital on October 15, 1958. Many things went through my mind as I drove Ann and Beth home from the hospital. I was determined to give her a better opportunity than I had experienced. I knew I loved her unconditionally. Ann and I were both very happy. The reality, however, was that we were two 20-year-old kids with a very questionable future.

Work was enjoyable and going well. I was responsible for all of the reconnaissance helicopter mechanics, the hand-to-hand combat training, and once a month, a warrant officer and I paid the troops. My only extra duty was to be in charge of quarters about once a month.

Another Specialist, Herman Smith, (not his real name) was responsible for the cargo helicopter mechanics. He had been a crew chief on B29's in World War II. He saw many difficult things over Europe and the Pacific. Without a doubt, he was the best aircraft mechanic I ever knew. He was bright and quick-witted. When I returned from getting married, he asked, "Why did you go and do such a dumb thing?" I laughed and replied, "Herman, why did you never marry? You couldn't find anyone who would have you?" His response, "Love is when two fools meet. Marriage is an institution, and I never wanted to be a part of a fool's institution."

His addiction to alcohol made his time in the army a roller coaster. He had been up and down the ranks many times. In the summer, he took leave on a three-day-pass. While there, he received his Korean War bonus. Unfortunately, he decided to drink it all up. He said he came home one night after midnight, and his mother asked why he was coming home so late. He replied, "Because it's the only place open."

He returned two weeks later from his three day leave. Being A.W.O.L. is a serious offense in the Army. Captain Loveland did not want to lose him as a mechanic. He demoted him one stripe and gave him two hours' extra duty for two weeks. All discipline of noncommissioned officers had to be reviewed by the battalion commander because only he could approve the demotion of a noncommissioned officer. On review it was decided that since Captain Loveland did not have the authority to demote him, he could not take away his rank. His punishment would have been ten hours' extra duty for being AWOL for two weeks. It was decided to transfer him to Thule, Greenland for a year. Unfortunately, on the day he was to leave, he got paid. I happened to be in charge of quarters that night. At 7:00 p.m. he came into the orderly room drunk. I asked to see his train ticket. He was to catch the train at 9:00 that evening and report to Fort Dix the next morning to fly to Greenland. I found a PFC and told him to use Capt. Loveland's jeep, take Specialist Smith to the train, and not come back until he saw him leave.

A year later I was driving through the company area and saw him wearing the rank of Specialist Two, a promotion. I asked what happened. He said that some Norwegians had been stuck on the ice. He and an air force pilot in a helicopter had rescued them. He had received a letter of appreciation from the military and his picture had been in a national news magazine. The next payday he went AWOL again, and the last time I saw him, he was back down to private. Sadly, I saw a lot of this in the army.

Herman was an interesting and tragic person, but there were also many healthy people in the military. Some were in to meet their obligation; others were making a career of it. Most of the people we related to were in for the two years required of them, or like me, had enlisted to go to a good military school.

We assumed I would finish my enlistment in the 582nd. It was a good place. This, however, was not to be. In late July, the captain paged me to his office. He instructed me to pick a group of men to bring every helicopter in the transportation school up to flight status. I chose ten mechanics and we began inspecting the helicopters assigned to the school. We pulled each one into a hanger for the repairs. We saved the one in the worst condition for last. The engine had to be completely disassembled and we replaced many of the parts.

Every day Capt. Jack Smith (not his real name) stopped by and asked questions about what we were doing. He was a Senior Army Aviator and in charge of the structure and rigging department of the school. As we were finishing, he asked "Is it going to run when you finish?" I replied, "Everyone we have worked on so far has." He was present the next morning when we pulled it out of the hanger to start the engine. Fortunately, the engine started the second time the starter turned it over. We tied all of the helicopters down and when I was discharged six months later, each was where we had left it.

Two weeks later, out of the blue, I was reassigned to the transportation school. The orders read I would be attached to the headquarters company, but would report to Captain Smith in the transportation school. I reported to him the next day. He assigned me a desk and told me he needed someone with my experience to teach.

One of the department's tasks was to train pilots who wanted to be maintenance officers. There were about 20 in each class. All were captains or majors hoping the school would increase their chances of promotion in the rapidly-growing aviation branch of the army. By now it was against army regulations for an enlisted man to teach officers. The next day I learned the real reason I had been reassigned. Captain Jack, which was what he liked to be called, began his workday with a cup of half bourbon and half coffee. By midmorning he was feeling no pain. Each day by noon I took over his class.

I continued the rest of my army time teaching the maintenance officers. Capt. Jack encouraged me to sign up for three more years, adding that he would get me promoted to E-5. I told him I really did not want to stay in the army. Then he offered me a job as a civilian in the department, which I also declined. He then began to recommend me for other jobs in aviation. He was a pilot in World War II, so he knew a lot of people. I expressed my profound appreciation for his efforts on my behalf but took him up on none of them.

Like a civilian school, the army transportation school practically shut down for Christmas. Each of the students was given a ten day leave. It was announced on the public address system that all of the students would assemble in our building and be addressed by the colonel in command of the school before going on leave. All of the instructors who were military had already gone on leave except Capt. Jack and me. By noon he was well into the spirits—and I do not mean the Christmas kind—and had gone home saying he was ill. When the colonel came, I was the ranking man present. I reported and told the colonel the students were present and ready for his speech.

His angry response was, "Where in the hell is Jack Smith?" My reply was, "The captain is at home ill." His response, "We know what his problem is, don't we?" I smiled and said, "If you say so, Colonel."

My last few days in the army were a time of personal struggle. I knew I had to support my family. A sure way to do that would be to re-enlist because we were making do nicely on my army pay. Re-enlisting would bring a bonus of several thousand dollars and a promotion. Yet deep down inside I knew, and Ann knew better than I, that I was being called into the ministry. Many ministers whom I had observed were somewhat feminine and I was very masculine. But I was neither good enough nor pious enough to be a minister. Super pious people made me want to cuss in their presence. Some had little ambition and I had many ambitions. Many were poor and I did not want to ever be poor again. On January 15, 1959, I was discharged from the army at Fort Eustis, Virginia. I received 30 days leave pay, so we had money and time to find a job.

REFLECTIONS ON ARMY EXPERIENCE

My three years in the army were God's preparation program for my ministry. In the army I had the chance to lead in positions not normally experienced by people my age. I had learned you were accountable to those who had authority over you and that you cared for those you led. I learned that one had to depend on the members of the group for support and completion of the mission. I learned that there was petty idle barracks gossip that was best ignored, and serious gossip that had to be dealt with. Most importantly, I learned to speak in public and hold the groups' attention. In the military I saw people from all walks of life, which made it clear that being different was neither good nor bad; it was just different. I saw clearly that every person was capable of good and bad—that no one is 100% saint or sinner.

A TIME AT SEARS

January 16, 1959 was my first day as a civilian. We liked living in our little house beside the screen of the Yorktown drive-in theater. Our landlord owned the theater, and we were allowed to watch the movies for free. Both Ann and I were still thinking about my entering the ministry. I did not know all of what would be involved in entering the ministry. My feelings were split. I thought if I got a good job, made a little money, and worked hard in church, the feelings of being called would go away.

On a Monday morning I went to the employment commission in Newport News, Virginia and was told times were hard and that I probably should re-enlist. Since I enjoyed being in the military, I entertained that as a possibility but it meant a three-year commitment. Still thinking of the ministry, I needed a job where I could give a brief notice and leave. So I parked my car at the end of the main retail street and started going from store to store looking for a sales job. Montgomery Ward had nothing. My next stop was the Sears store. It was an old narrow three story building. After I filled out the paperwork and was interviewed by the personnel manager, he offered me a job selling paint and auto parts. The base pay was more than my army salary, and with commissions if I did well, I would be earning about 25% more. I began the following Monday.

We decided to visit our family in the days prior to my starting work. Kate, Ann's mother, told us soon after we arrived that she had gotten me a factory job, and we could live with her until we had enough money to rent an apartment. Ann and I had decided earlier that it was better for both of us to not return home, but to stay where we were. We thanked her and told her I had the job at Sears and enough money to last until I got my first paycheck.

Since I had entered the military before I was old enough to register for the draft, I had to register for the draft within thirty days of my discharge. I had completed my required active duty, so there was almost no possibility that I would be drafted. On the second day we were home I went to the courthouse to register. The clerk of the court, Billy Sandiedge, was also the clerk of the draft board. He was a longtime friend of Ann's mother and had been like a father to Ann. He truly was a fine and wise man. He asked me where we planned to live and what I planned to do. I told him about the job at Sears but not about our interest in ministry. Then he made a most remarkable comment. "Do what you love and the money will take care of itself." It was beginning to dawn on me that good advice often comes unexpectedly. When it does, meditate on it, implement it in your life, and when the opportunity comes, share it with others. To this day I have never forgotten that profound statement. I have shared it with many people and observed that those who have a passion for what they do rarely have financial problems. They also see work as play and achieve great things.

On Sunday afternoon we returned to our little house by the drive-in theater. The next morning, Ann packed my lunch and I put on my only sport coat and tie and set out to be a salesman. The store was open on Monday and Friday nights and everybody worked all day Saturday. I soon learned the joke that the only way to be off on Saturday was to quit on Friday. On my first day, a customer put a good shock into me. When I asked him if I could help him, he gruffly said, "Young man, do I look like I need help?" From then on, I never approached a customer with that comment.

Work went well and I learned a lot about paint and auto parts. My sales were enough that my commission added 20% to my pay. The sales people often talked of the new modern store Sears was building several blocks away. On Saturday afternoon of my fifth week, the personnel manager, Ed Beck, telephoned the department and said he wanted to see me in his office. I walked up the three flights of stairs wondering if I was going to be fired or assigned to another department.

As I entered his office, he told me to have a seat. He began by saying he had been observing me with customers and that I had sold more than anyone else in the two departments. He continued that the new store would have all of the departments of a full store and would be the most modern Sears store in the country. Further, some of the department managers would continue in the new store, but no one here had any experience with soft lines, clothes, bedding, etc., so all of those managers would be new. He said, "There's one slot left. It's the bath and linen department. The store manager and I have talked and if you feel you can do it, we want to promote you to manager of that department with a substantial raise." I readily accepted. He explained that three others had been promoted that day as well. All of us were to begin division manager's training for two weeks on Monday at the Norfolk, Virginia store. He had asked one of the others to drive, and we were to carpool. When the store opened, all of us would be expected to wear suits. The company would give us a 50% discount, and we should buy at least two suits while we were in the Norfolk store.

I went home on cloud nine. Here I was, not 21 years old yet. My military obligation was behind me. I had a good job and a good, loving, supportive wife and a great daughter. What more could a young man want?

The assigned driver lived nearby so he picked me up on Monday morning, and we started training. In a classroom they explained what our jobs would be. We would meet once a month in Norfolk with the merchandising manager, order stock, and plan promotions. We were taught how to handle checks, returns, the soon-to-be-introduced Sears credit card, and how to teach the salespeople to count a section of stock on counter each morning, so we could order what we needed. We were taught that the customer comes first. If we had more customers than we could handle, we were to call the store manager and he would come and help.

When we finished our training, we went to the new store and interviewed from a pool of people the personnel manager had pre-screened for jobs in the store. I chose two full-time workers and two part-time. The full-time workers and I set up the displays and stocked the counters. The grand opening was on a Thursday since the new store would be open Thursday and Friday evenings and continue through Saturday.

When the new store opened, there were hundreds of customers waiting at the doors. We had the first gourmet candy department in that part of the state. The choices included fried grasshoppers and chocolate-covered ants and the department was overwhelmed. The president of Sears was present at the opening. When he saw customers waiting, he rolled up his sleeves and sold candy for a couple of hours. A customer asked, "What job do you have with the store?" He modestly replied, "I am president of Sears." The customer later told a hardware salesman, "You have some weird people working here. That guy over there tried to get me to believe he is the president of Sears." When the salesman replied, "He is," the customer shook his head and exited the store. To me it was obvious why, at the time, Sears was the largest retailer in the world and growing every day. The leader believed his job was to do whatever it took to get the job done.

We had been attending the Deer Park Baptist Church which was meeting in an elementary school. As soon as it was clear we were going to remain in the area, we joined the church on the last Sunday it was in the school. Shortly after moving into the new church building, Joe Strother, the pastor, asked me to start a young couples' class. Ann and I pitched in and soon there was a group of 15 to 20 each Sunday. I enjoyed the teaching and thought maybe this would be enough. I also made house calls on prospects with the pastor on my day off. Many evenings Ann and I discussed the ministry. We both prayed probably every day about what we should do. We could not figure out a way to be able to afford to go to school.

The job went extremely well. The store manager, Charles Ashmore, was a Baptist deacon and many of the employees were Christians. The manager for the Tidewater group was J.J. Garia. He had started in the stockroom and came up through the ranks to the top position. Similar to leaders I had known in the army, he had an interest in those who worked for him, particularly his junior managers. While we were in managers' school, he met privately with each of us.

The meeting with him was very personal in nature. He asked about where and how we grew up. He inquired about our families and our goals. Whenever he visited our store, he visited each department and asked how things were going.

When he did, he asked about our wives and children by name before he talked business. You soon learned to always tell him the truth because he checked your department sales and profit before he came to see you.

One day when he was in the store, I was checking my stockroom and rearranging stock for an upcoming sale. Mr. Garia walked through on his way to see the stock manager. He stopped and spoke to me and asked, "Allen, are you straightening up your stockroom?" Then he went on, "We are paying you to be a manager not a stock boy. I do not want to see you doing this again. We pay people to do this and if you keep doing it, some stock boy will lose his job. Further, we hired you to manage your department. Now if you want to work in the stockroom, I can arrange that, but I will also have to cut your pay." He walked away, and I found a stock boy and told him what I needed done. His words made me angry, but I held my tongue. On reflection he was right, leaders assign and delegate work. The words "If you want a job done right, do it yourself" are the motto of a poor leader.

Everything was going extremely well. We were both working very hard in church, but deep inside, we both felt that we were running from God just as Jonah did in Scripture. One evening in July we were talking over supper. Beth was contentedly playing with her food in her highchair. Ann looked me in the eye and said, "I am disappointed in you. You don't have faith at all. You think you have to work this all out yourself. If you apply to seminary, don't you believe God will help you? I believe that." I was shocked, but that night I wrote a letter to the director of admissions at Southeastern Seminary.

In about a week, his reply came. The letter stated that they would love to have me as a student at their school, but I had to have a college degree prior to entering. The director suggested I apply at the University of Richmond. That night we wrote a letter to the university requesting an application. When it arrived, I filled it out and sent it in. In three weeks I received the letter of acceptance without any mention of my poor high school record. The dean, Dr. Robert Smart, said that I would receive a full semester's credit for my military service and since I was preparing for the ministry, my tuition would be free. He suggested that I apply for Virginia Baptist ministerial assistance which would more than cover my other college fees. He also advised that it was too late to apply for the first semester, but later, I was likely to receive a scholarship from the Charles Keese Fund.

Ann was right. If you take that first step of faith, God will help you. In less than a month I was accepted into college and given a plan to have all of my school expenses paid. Yet there were many things left for us to do. How would we pay the rent and eat? We had some money, but we were short about $300 of what was needed to pay a rent deposit and live until we found a job. School would start the Tuesday after Labor Day. We wanted to be there a week early to find a job.

Shortly after my acceptance, we went home to tell our mothers. Ann's mother had trouble believing we were going to attempt such a thing, but she agreed to co-sign a note for the 300 dollars we needed. One of the banks that had refused me a loan to continue at Virginia Tech loaned us the money.

The last week in August we moved into our apartment at 206 N. Harrison Street. We furnished it with any furniture anyone would give us. I found a job as an aide at Tuckers Mental Hospital working 3:00 p.m. to 11:00 p.m. The day before classes started, I interviewed for and received the Virginia Baptist Aid for Ministerial Students. While I was standing in line, I met Ernie Boyd who became my best friend for over 40 years.

REFLECTIONS ON MY TIME AT SEARS

At Sears it became clear to me that one cannot be happy regardless of how successful one might be if one is in fact running from what God wants a person to do. Nevertheless, God may be equipping you for an assignment that he has for you later. What I learned at Sears were skills that enabled me to earn money to later stay in seminary. He was also introducing me to some more good leaders. Sometimes God's words come to you through those who care about you. In this case God spoke through my wife, Ann.

THE UNIVERSITY

After a week's orientation, classes began. Today the campus is one of the most beautiful in the country. When I was a student, the schools that were primarily male were on a low hill and Westhampton, the college for women, was on another hill separated by a lake. Freshmen were required to park on the Westhampton side of the college. On our second morning of classes, Ernie and I met in the parking lot. We walked down the hill by the chapel and across the dam for the lake. At the end of the dam, we were met by two upperclassmen who were football players. Ernie was a navy veteran, a good size fellow, and a great athlete. I was 6 feet, 2 inches tall and a lean 200 pounds. The tradition during orientation was that upperclassmen throw freshmen into the lake. They informed us that it had been brought to their attention that we had missed out on that privilege. Ernie reached out his hand to shake hands and said, "The last fellow that took me on ended up in the hospital. Allen, here, is a former army hand-to-hand combat instructor." Turning to me he said, "Which one do you want to take? Be careful you don't kill him—just break his collarbone—that ought to end his football career." In unison, the tough football players, said, "Lighten up, we're only kidding," and walked away. They were appreciative of us not telling the story around campus. We felt that it would be unseemly to spread rumors about two ministerial students threatening two football players.

The faculty had outstanding teachers and most of them were churchmen. A few were old school, and they thought their job was to intimidate the student and motivate him with the threat of a failing grade. My biology professor was of that persuasion. He began the course by telling us all the things that would cost us a point on our final grade. The most bizarre was if we left our lab chair out after class. My second day I was a minute late to class. He looked at his watch and said, "You are late, that will cost you a point on the next test." I felt like I was back in basic training. If I had been, I would have asked him to meet me behind the barracks. Things got worse. My midterm came back with a big red F. All of the answers were correct, but he took off points for each misspelled word. He handed me my paper and suggested I consider dropping the class. I kept my mouth shut and had Ann call out the words over and over until I could spell them. I ended up with a D, but I got a C in the second semester.

On the other hand, my Latin professor, W. W. Hackley, was just the opposite. He began the first day with, "I have checked your records. You may be the best class I have ever taught. It would not surprise me if all of you made A's." When one of us missed a word, he would smile and say, "I am surprised a man of your caliber missed that." What we heard was, "he thinks I am a person of real caliber." So we studied to confirm his opinion of us. Rarely did anyone fail in his class. He loved and believed in students. In our second year of Latin when he was 70 years old, he changed the book to make it easier on us. I made an A along with about half the class. The words I wrote in a poem years later are true. "I am not what you think I am; I am what I think you think I am."

Spelling was and is still difficult for me. The English department gave all incoming freshmen a spelling test on the 100 most commonly misspelled words. I missed 55 of them. In one essay, I misspelled shepherd. Dr. Peple, a wonderful teacher, wrote on my paper, "Allen, as a minister, you are going to need to know how to spell shepherd." Like a third grader, I wrote those spelling words over and over until I could spell them correctly.

During first semester it appeared that I would be lucky to make it through. In part, I was exhausted a great deal of the time. I was working the 3-11 shift at the hospital and had an 8 o'clock class six days a week. In October, Ann stepped up to bat and said I needed to study more and that she was going to work. This was a hard decision for Ann as our daughter, Beth, was a few weeks less than a year old. She got a job at the Department of Motor Vehicles earning enough to pay the bills. Her job also provided healthcare. One of the saddest days of this period was the day I put Beth in a daycare so that her mother could work. A second was the day I pawned my army uniforms to buy us milk.

It seems to me that when you set out to follow God—just as Pharaoh was hot on the heels of the chosen people when they fled Egypt—evil, or whatever you choose to call it—the devil is fine with me—is nipping at your heels. We got slapped upside the head big time.

Ann was visiting her mother, hit a slick spot in the road, and wrecked our old Dodge. The car was totaled. Fortunately she only had minor injuries. So we had to buy another car which we could not afford. The used car was a lemon, so we only kept it a couple of months. Then we had a miscarriage.

At the end of the semester, I was beginning to believe the story frequently told of an early country student who came to the university to study for the ministry. He managed to fail every subject. Dr. Cousins, the icon of religion professors in Virginia, called him in to discuss his call to the ministry. The student said he had been plowing corn, and he saw in the clouds the letters P-C. He knew that meant he was to preach Christ. Dr. Cousins asked, "Son, did you ever think it could have meant plow corn." I was beginning to think I should have stayed in the army or at Sears.

When the semester ended, I had at least survived. I had made one A, Two B's, one C and one D. I certainly was a long way from being a good student.

When I registered for the second semester, I decided to take Psychology of Religion with Dr. O.W. Rhodenhiser. It was a small class and a fascinating course. Before the first month was out, he asked me to come to his office as soon as I finished my classes for the day. I expected his advice would be that I was probably not going to make it. The absolute opposite was true. He began our conversation by saying I had an excellent mind and gave good answers in class. My problem was that I did poorly putting my answers on paper. To my surprise, he assured me he would help me with the problem and suggested that I talk with my other teachers. I am sure when I left his office I had to wipe the tears from my eyes. From then on I took every class he taught and he became a lifelong friend and mentor. My fourth book is dedicated to Dr. Rhodenhiser.

Things were improving. Ann's working took most of the money pressure off. We also found a student's wife who would babysit Beth. I received a generous scholarship from the Keese fund for the second semester. The Y.M.C.A. also gave me a two-afternoon-a-week job as a Gray Y leader in a school for underprivileged children. This job entailed going to the school and organizing boys into football and baseball teams. Our goal was to teach them Christian values through sports.

In January I was approached by another student asking me if I wanted to preach in his place at the Elko Community Church. He had been called to another small church as pastor. I eagerly accepted. The Sunday after I preached they called me as pastor. That meant $50 more per month and an opportunity to be a pastor. It was fun, funny and frustrating all at the same time.

First, when you serve a small church, you are not the leader; you are the chaplain to the families of the church. Trying to lead is like trying to herd cats. One of the leaders was a man in his 80's that everyone called Uncle Tom. He smoked a pipe, but did not want me to know it. After a deacons' meeting, he thought I had left for home. The deacons were standing behind the church. I remembered I needed to ask the chairman something. When I walked up, Uncle Tom put his lit pipe in his pocket. I exited as quickly as I could to prevent him from setting himself on fire.

One Sunday I was preaching a sermon on the Good Samaritan. I described how easy it was to be on the wrong side of the road and how it took courage to cross over and help someone in the ditch. Uncle Tom jumped up and shouted. "Amen, you tell them, preacher."

The little church grew as subdivisions developed around it. In a business meeting they were discussing building additional Sunday school rooms. A young couple suggested that they borrow the money and build them now. Ethel, an elderly lady, the wife of George, a deacon, responded, "You can borrow all the money you want, but George is not going to sign any notes." George jumped to his feet and said, "I will too, Ethel!" The rooms were built.

The church wrote a letter to my home church asking that I be licensed to preach. My home church responded that they would like to have me ordained. Usually, Baptist ministers are ordained when they enter seminary. I went before the ordination council of the Piedmont Baptist Association. They voted to support my ordination.

On Sunday, April 20, 1960, the Emmanuel Baptist Church, Sandiedges, Virginia, held my ordination ceremony. The pastor, L.L. Schweimer presided over the service. He had baptized me in Big Piney River when I was 15 years old and had been a great encourager in my life. He did something I had never heard of before or since. When the time for the laying on of hands came, he said, "We are really setting apart two people for ministry, Ray and Ann. I want Ann to come and kneel beside Ray, and we will lay hands on her as well." Every ordained minister and deacon laid hands on both of us.

Back at the university, intramural sports were very popular. Each organization in the men's college fielded a softball team including the ministerial association. Some of the groups recruited heavily from the baseball and football team. Most teams saw a game against the ministerial association team as an easy win. That spring, however, there were many veterans on campus. The leaders of the team of ministers were Ernie Boyd, my friend, who had played semi-pro ball and pitched a softball at over 80 miles per hour; Harvey Skinner, who had been a catcher on a military team; and Dr. L. D. Johnson, the head of the religion department, who had gone to college on a baseball scholarship. That spring the team of ministers—to the embarrassment of the "he men" college athletes—went undefeated. My perception of ministers being effeminate was being laid to rest. Since Ernie's and my encounter with two football players and the team's championship, athletes were becoming very friendly with the ministerial students. They certainly were not going to cross any of the vets.

The first semester at the university had been a time of testing. The second was a time of confirmation. With the help of my professors and Ann's calling out questions before every test and proofreading my papers, my grades came up. Three A's and two C's.

That summer I decided to take a break from school and work. I got a job selling hardware at the Sears in Southside Plaza. It was a good summer—I sold a load of tools. I repaired the lawnmowers customers had trouble with. Often a simple carburetor adjustment fixed them. The store manager was a Baptist and active in his local church. At the end of the summer, he asked me if I would come back the next summer and work as each manager went on vacation. I agreed.

School started in the fall. Since I liked my course in psychology of religion, I signed up for another psychology course and one in sociology. Probably because of my background, I thought these courses would help me gain more self-understanding. This turned out to be true. I began to see how the culture of the hollow where I grew up and the accepted psychological understanding of the community had shaped me and my neighbors.

I also took Logic. My mother had always been critical of me, saying I was born asking why, and what I needed to do was accept that she knew best. In high school, math was one of my better subjects and I loved playing with figures. I often figured different ways to solve a problem, but it was wrong unless I did it the teacher's way. One day in class I asked the teacher, "If someone were standing in New York and another in Florida, would the man in Florida be going faster because of the rotation of the earth?" She ridiculed me and said they are both attached to the earth and had to be going the same speed. The first day in logic class, the professor gave us an intuitive logic test. The next day, the professor, David White, called me aside and said I made the highest score that anyone in his classes had ever made. He taught us symbolic logic. He also took an interest in me and suggested additional exercises to increase my abilities. On the final exam I made 100%. The course helped me understand better that some of my childhood frustration was because of how my brain worked.

I had taken college algebra in the army and made an A, so I was allowed to take trigonometry in college. Dr. Clarence Monk was the professor. He was a gifted teacher and encouraged us to figure many ways to solve a problem. He took a great interest in me and encouraged me to take more math, which I could not do and also take the courses I needed to attend seminary. Both he and Professor White became lifelong friends. To the surprise of my department head when I took the graduate record exam at graduation, my scores in the social sciences and math were my highest.

By now I loved the university and its teachers. They were great. They repeatedly emphasized that the Richmond man was a thinking man. I majored in religion but took extra courses in the social sciences and philosophy.

Shortly before Thanksgiving, Bethany Place Baptist Church, a suburban church in Richmond, approached me about becoming their associate pastor and preaching at a mission they had started in an underprivileged neighborhood. My professors in the religion department advised me to take the job because it would give me some experience in a larger church. The old house the mission was meeting in had burned down the previous spring. Due to limited funds, the church voted not to continue the mission but to try to get more people to come to Bethany Place. They also asked me to continue in the role of associate pastor and work with the youth. I agreed. Because of cultural differences, the people of the mission did not come to the mother church but went elsewhere or quit church altogether. Birds of a feather do in fact flock together. People are always more comfortable with people like themselves. I began to see that culture may be a bigger factor affecting people coming to a church than the church wanted to admit.

The most important thing that happened there was that I met one of the most remarkable lay people I ever knew. Walter N. Johnson owned the J and J supermarket. He never refused a poor person food. The churches often had him fill their food baskets for the poor. He always added a six-pack of Pepsi and some candy. When good church people complained, his response was "Poor children like Pepsi and candy just like your children. I donate the drinks and candy. If you don't like it, go somewhere else."

He and his Sunday school class helped many ministerial students at the university and in seminary. While we were seminary students, it seemed that just when we needed it most, a check from his class would arrive.

He also had a good sense of humor and little patience with Christian stupidity. One night during a church revival, the evangelist could not get anyone to come forward. After far too many verses of "Just as I Am," Mr. Johnson went forward and rededicated his life. Most of the church was shocked at this.

The next day I went by his store and asked. "Walter, what on Earth were you doing last night?" Laughing he said, "I had an order of meat coming this morning, and I was afraid if somebody did not go forward, I would not be here to let the delivery man in. Besides, God does not call preachers to beg people into the kingdom, and I try to rededicate my life to God every day. This time I just did it in public, and everybody got to go home and go to bed at a decent hour."

It was a privilege to name our youngest daughter after him (Kathleen Johnson Allen). Much later when Ann inherited some money from her Aunt Ford Whitehead, she endowed the Walter Johnson Scholarship for Ministerial Students at the University of Richmond.

Meanwhile, my work with the Y.M.C.A. was going well. The boys in the Gray Y club were teaching me a lot. A big part of the program was ball teams that competed in a city-wide Y.M.C.A. league. In the spring, our boys went to the final game of the playoffs. Each day at the end of practice, we had devotion and one of the boys led in prayer. Ed wanted with all of his heart to pitch. He had excellent ability, and in practice, pitched well. The problem was every time I started Ed, he walked four boys and had to be pulled from the game. At our last practice he asked to say the prayer. To say the least, he took the scripture, "Ask and you will receive," literally. His prayer, "Oh, Lord, make Ray let me pitch Saturday and give me control." At first I thought I should say something, but I didn't. In fact his prayer troubled me. So figuring we were going to lose anyway, I started him. He pitched a no-hitter and we won the championship. I still think about it. Did my decision calm him down to where he could do his best and encourage the rest of the team to do their best? Or does God hear and care about a ten-year-old boy's prayers? I still choose to believe God hears, cares about, and answers prayers.

I finished the semester with greatly-improved grades. To graduate in three years as planned, I had to take my first year of a second language in order to complete a second year in two languages. On the advice of my faculty adviser, I took

German. One professor thought that you should learn to speak German. The other thought you ought to be able to read German well. I drew Dr. Skinner, a World War II translator. He thought he was still in the army because he beat the desk with his cane every time you mispronounced a German word. I missed so many, I felt sorry for his desk. All of his tests were English to German translation. I was thankful to receive a C. The second semester I had to take the professor who stressed reading. All of his instruction was from German to English. My D kept me off the Dean's list my senior year.

My German class was at 8:00 a.m. George Tapscott, the Sears store manager, let me come to work at 11:00 so that I could work full time and get a little money saved up for my senior year. I also wanted very much to buy a class ring and purchase Ann a University of Richmond friendship ring. They both cost about $200. When we saved up the money, I went to the school and ordered both rings. The day the rings came was a very happy day. We had both worked very hard to stay at the university. With the rings on our fingers, the end was in sight. Ann's ring acknowledged her great contribution to my being able to complete college.

That summer I worked in each manager's place when he went on vacation. By now most of the people in the store were comfortable with working with a ministerial student. Many women shopped in our store. It seemed that the ladies with the skinniest-fitting halter tops often came to me. When they would lean over to sign a check or credit card, their breasts were in plain view. Often after assisting these ladies, another salesman would come up and say, "Ray, did you see that set of knockers? It would be nice to lay your head on those." Some would ask, "Does that bother you?" My response always would be, "I am not blind, and they do not castrate you when you are ordained."

Two historic events happened in Richmond that summer. Students from Virginia Union protested at the Woolworth lunch counter. It was discussed on campus, but none of our students joined in the protest. It took many more years, but today America's opportunities are open to all of its citizens. The second event was that the first fast food hamburger restaurant opened across the street from our store. It was a Kelley's serving hamburgers with catsup and onions for 15 cents and cheeseburgers for 17 cents. Both events changed the world. Fast food is America's gift to the world. Thus far no nations having a McDonald's have fought each other.

In the fall of 1961, I began my senior year at the university. That year was a busy time. I needed to take six courses each semester, and write my senior paper which had to answer ten questions and be at least fifty pages long. Fortunately I was able to schedule all of my classes in the morning, and half of them were in the religion department.

Each day there was a half hour break after required chapel. Dr. L. D. Johnson invited the upperclassmen to his office for coffee during the 30-minute break before classes started. He asked about our plans and shared stories of his experience at the First Baptist Church of Danville, Virginia, where he had served for twenty years before becoming head of the religion department.

Dr. Ted Adams, pastor of the First Baptist Church of Richmond and president of the Baptist World Alliance, came frequently to campus and spoke to the ministerial association. He had traveled the world. All of us had dreams of being pastors and doing what these men had none. Yet deep down I thought with my background that the best I could hope for was a small church.

Southeastern Seminary was the smallest and newest seminary the Southern Baptists had at that time. Since it was only 100 miles from Richmond, I decided I would go there. Most believed that Southern Seminary, where all of my teachers had gone, was the most scholarly and one of the best seminaries in the world. I never really thought of going there. In early February, I filled out the application for Southeastern but never sent it in.

In late February Dr. Johnson told me he wanted to see me in private. In his office he told me he had been thinking about me a lot, and that I should not go to Southeastern, but Southern. Further, he had nominated me for a scholarship and that we should plan to stay there through a doctorate. I told him I needed to think about it and talk it over with my wife. He handed me an application. Ann and I both agreed if that's what Dr. Johnson thought we should do, then we should do it. I sent the application in and was accepted, but someone else got the scholarship.

Two incidents happened in the church that semester that made me think a couple of things through. In the church there was a very active young couple. He owned a successful small business. He also was the youngest deacon in the church. They worked tirelessly to make their house a show place. They made an appointment to talk with me about their marriage. With the wife in tears, they shared he wanted a divorce. I saw them several times and tried my best to get them to give it another chance. On the fourth session they said they were going through with the divorce, but they both appreciated my help and their last act together was that they had bought me a beautiful Hamilton watch to thank me. I still have the watch today. My lesson was you cannot talk people into doing what they do not want to do. You can only share your thoughts about their situation. They are responsible for the results.

The second incident happened on a Sunday afternoon. When church was over, a woman was sitting in a pew crying. The pastor asked me to talk with her. She poured out her story of how her husband had threatened to kill her if she did not stop criticizing him. She maintained all she wanted was to save their marriage and for him to stop drinking. Having grown up in a home where weekend drinking and fussing and fighting were a regular event, I recognized that part of the violence level could have been avoided if my mother had not tried to correct a drunken man's faults. So I told her if she really did want to save her marriage, I would go visit her husband. She claimed it would not be safe because he had a gun and might shoot me. I was still young and remembered how to disarm a man from my army training, so I knocked on his door. The husband, Frank, opened the door and asked, "Who in the hell are you?" I told him who I was and that his wife had asked my advice, but that I wanted to hear his side before I gave her advice. His response, "Come on in. You are the first damn preacher I ever met that had any sense." He spent an hour admitting he did have a temper, that he usually drank one six pack a weekend, and he was tired of her calling him a drunk. It was clear to me he had been drinking but was not intoxicated. There was a .38 police special on the coffee table. I assured him I would be happy to talk with both of them, left and did not hear from either of them again.

Ten years later when I was serving the Cosby Memorial Baptist Church in Richmond as pastor, my phone rang at home one evening. The caller asked if I were the preacher at Bethany Place in the sixties. I affirmed I was. He said,

"This is Frank. You came to my door and I called you a damn preacher." "Sure, I remember," I said. "Well," he said, "I divorced that woman and remarried a real Christian lady. I have been converted and now am a deacon in the Fairmont Baptist Church. I just wanted to call you and thank you for listening to my side." Through the years, many women have come for help. Sometimes the conflict has gone too far to resolve. There really is little hope if the husband does not come too. Most wives said their husbands would not come to counseling. With the wife's permission, I often wrote a simple letter to the husband to the effect that his wife had come to see me seeking help for the marriage. I then told the husband that it would help me if he would come and share how he saw things. I have never had a husband that did not respond and come to counseling. For many that was the step that saved the marriage or helped with a peaceful divorce.

I was unaware that the leader of our state convention knew who I was. The executive director of the Baptist General Association, Dr. Lucius Pohill, often came to the campus and talked with the students. In May, he telephoned me and said churches all over Virginia called him to find a preacher to fill in for their pastor's vacation. He said he would like to send me every Sunday to one of those churches. He assured me they would pay me and include some travel expenses. I readily agreed to it and thanked him for the opportunity.

Unfortunately, my car was not in good shape. One day I was talking with Walter Johnson about his new car. He said I should trade cars soon so I would have reliable transportation to go to seminary. He told me to arrange a trade and he would help me. With his help I was able to buy a new 1961 Plymouth Valiant for $1,795. He helped with the down payment, enabling me to have a $50 per month car payment. The car never gave me a problem while in seminary and well into my first church. My lovely three-year-old daughter christened the car with raw peanut barf.

Graduating from the University of Richmond was a moving event for me. When I walked off the stage with my degree, I was the first person in my family to have a degree. It felt great.

I resigned from Bethany Place Church and returned to Sears to fill in for each manager. Every Sunday morning we got up early and drove the two or three hours to the church we were speaking in. This was a great experience which introduced me to more than a dozen churches in the eastern part of the state.

At the end of the summer, George Gray (another student attending Southern) and I rented a U-Haul truck for the trip. When we finished packing and loading the truck, I doubt there was room for a single pan. The evening after we finished packing, we drove home for Labor Day weekend to visit with family.

A friend of Ann's stepfather had a small pond in the town. He told me I could fish in it if I liked. I had started fishing with a willow pole and a bent straight pin when I was five years old. Since that time I rarely missed the chance to go fishing. At the hardware store, the clerk sold me the latest lure, a rubber artificial worm. I caught several bass on that bait and over 50 years later, an artificial worm is still my favorite bass bait.

Early Tuesday morning we started our journey to Southern Seminary in Louisville, Kentucky. The interstate system had not been built in many places in 1962 so it was a long ride. Ann drove our car, George drove his car and I drove the truck. Beth, our daughter, rode the truck with me in her car seat. We had to drive down Main Street in the small towns of southwest Virginia, then over crazy, crooked two-lane roads through the mountains. When the time came for us to switch and for George to drive the truck, his wife had become ill and I had to drive the whole trip. In the late afternoon, we stopped at a motel. They wanted to charge George extra for his two daughters to sleep on the floor, and he asked that we drive to the next town. Fortunately, at the next town, Mt. Sterling, Kentucky, the motel let his children stay free. We reached the seminary Wednesday before noon.

REFLECTIONS ON THE UNIVERSITY OF RICHMOND.

The University was and continues to be a great place to receive a good education. I am ever grateful for how it changed me. In the total scheme of life, however, I learned that life itself is a schoolhouse and every person you meet is your teacher. The lessons I learned from the professors and fellow students outside the classroom are perhaps as important as the formal classroom setting.

It is also one of the great miracles of life that when you need an encouraging word, God puts someone there to say it. There is an old proverb that states, "When the student is ready, the teacher appears." That happened over and over in my three years at the university. The teachers were: Dr. Bill Rhodenhiser and L.D. Johnson, my religion professors; Dr. W.W. Hackley, my Latin professor; Dr. Clarence Monk, my math professor; high school dropout grocery store owner and life guide, Walter N. Johnson; classmate and loyal and encouraging friend, Ernie Boyd; and my wife, Ann, who called out my spelling words.

SEMINARY

We arrived in St. Matthews, a suburb of Louisville, shortly before noon. Before reaching the seminary, we stopped at White Castle, one of the earlier fast food places that had 20-cent cheeseburgers. Things were more expensive there than in Virginia. For supper that night we bought fried chicken at Sander's, which was the first Kentucky Fried Chicken restaurant.

Our apartment was a wreck. The manager of Seminary Village, where most of the married students lived, was managed by a former small loan company manager. Even though the seminary owned the housing, the administration left the management to him. The paint was peeling, there were several holes in the walls, and the walls in the kitchen were dirty with grease. When I called this to his attention, his attitude was 'take it or leave it.' We had no choice but to take it. Our first few days were spent cleaning and painting. This colored in a negative way our attitude toward the seminary administration.

On Friday of that week I registered for classes which started the following Monday. We had planned for me not to work so that I could get a good start. I also planned to get the required Greek and Hebrew out of the way my first year. The Greek class was full when I got in line to register, so I registered for Hebrew. Dr. Donald Williams was the professor. The students called him "Diamond Don" behind his back because he came from a wealthy family and wore several expensive rings.

When I returned to our apartment, a senior living downstairs asked me what courses I had signed up for and who was teaching them. I had Dr. Ray Brown for New Testament survey and Dr. Williams for Hebrew. He told me both were mistakes. He said, "Dr. Brown will work you to death and most were lucky to get a C in his class." With great confidence he said, "It is impossible to pass Hebrew. Drop the class and take it with Dr. Owens next semester." The next morning at 8:00 a.m., I was in the registrar's office trying to drop the classes. He would not permit it.

Meanwhile, we put Beth in the seminary preschool and Ann went job hunting. The preschool was excellent. I took her each morning and picked her up after class. She played or napped while I studied in the afternoon. Ann found a job at the Dickinson Typesetting Company, where she worked as a proofreader.

What the senior had told me about Dr. Brown and Dr. Williams was true. They did work the students very hard, but both were always prepared and excellent teachers. Dr. Brown felt part of his job was to separate the average students from the better students. It also culled the lazy students from the class because several did not take him for the second semester. He required all of his students to memorize 100 verses of scripture each semester and tested us regularly to see that we could recite the assigned verses. He had read most of the books written about the New Testament. He had picked the most significant part of the book and assigned it for reading each day. We had to write a brief summary of what the author had written. He took up those notebooks and checked each summary. At the end of the second semester, my notebook had over 400 pages. I still have it and sometimes check things in it. He gave a midterm and a final exam. Each had one question from the reading and one from his lectures. When we asked how to review for his tests, his response always was, "Know it all and you will do fine." Dr. Williams was equally hard. Both men turned out to be two of the best teachers I had in seminary. I earned a B+ in both of their classes. Later, Dr. Brown was my doctoral supervisor.

My first year in seminary was a disappointing experience in many ways. At Richmond all my tests had been essay and you were encouraged to add your own thoughts in your answer. Here the way to make an A was to write what was in the books, what the professor had said in the lectures, and add nothing. Soon the good students were getting together to study. We made summaries of the readings and professor's lectures and shared study guides for tests with each other.

In February I went for an interview and trial sermon at the Lick Branch Baptist Church, Deputy, Indiana. It was a rural church of farmers with around 100 in attendance each Sunday. They were looking for someone to work only on Sundays. The pastor drove up Sunday morning, preached and visited the sick in the afternoon, spoke at Sunday night services, and returned to the seminary.

On my first trial Sunday, we went to Ernest Nay's house for lunch. After the meal he explained that several people would arrive shortly and they would like to ask me some questions. I thought they would ask about my beliefs. There were two questions. First, "Did I grow up in the city or country?" My response, "I grew up a mile and a half from the highway on a dirt road." Second question, "Are you an only child?" My response, "No, I am the oldest of ten children." He replied,

"That's fine, you will do." That ended the interview. He asked if I could come next Sunday and talk with another group.

After I got to know him better, I was in his barn talking with him one evening while he milked his cow and I asked why they only asked those two questions. He said, "We had a pastor once who was an only child and he thought he had to have his own way all the time. That was just not going to happen in our church. We also had a pastor from the city once. He even drove a city car and he didn't get along with country people." Politely I asked, "What is a city car?" He said, "A Dodge. Everybody knows a Dodge is a city car." Thankfully, I drove a Plymouth.

Throughout its history, this church had always had a student from the seminary as pastor. They had never had a full-time pastor. Many churches in the south have full-time pastors with a smaller attendance than this church had. The student before me had graduated and decided to move to the community and be the full-time pastor. Under his leadership the church had grown. They built a nice addition of six Sunday school rooms and a fellowship hall in the basement. The church sanctuary was heated by two old floor furnaces which came on with a loud boom. He attempted to persuade them to purchase a central heating system that would heat the new space and the sanctuary. The disagreement became so heated they fired him.

In my first week I heard the story several times and several different versions of it. After about a month, they asked what I thought should be done about the furnace. I told them I did not care. I had grown up in a house heated by a tin heater. If they wanted a tin heater in each room, that was fine with me. They bought the central furnace. It was a great place for a young pastor to learn.

All of the members were farmers. Some had additional jobs to support the farm. The wives kept the books and looked after the family finances. All of the deacons were men, but I soon learned that they would not make a decision if it involved money. Then it occurred to me that they were discussing all their farm finances with their wives before they decided if they could afford to proceed. So I brought up the church business one Sunday, told them to think and pray about it, and the next Sunday we would decide. Things went very smoothly after that.

In the spring, school was going better than the first semester. I was in the study group with the excellent students and my grades soon reflected that. I liked Hebrew, so I took the advanced course with Dr. J.J. Owens. It was a small class and he announced that all the work would be oral translation. We would translate portions of the book of Isaiah each day in class and come to his office and translate for the final exam. At the midterm he gave us a card with a midterm grade and a note from him. My card was B/A. The note said, "You should consider getting a doctorate in Old Testament." When I went to his office to translate, I was nervous. He told me to translate a verse. I mistranslated a word and knew it. He stopped me and said go to another verse. That verse had the word I had missed in it. I got it right that time and made no more mistakes. As I left he said, "When you corrected your mistake, you went from B to A."

Our money situation, however, was declining rapidly. So I went to Sears and applied for a job. The personnel manager interviewed me and told me what they paid part-time help, which was less than they paid in Richmond. I thanked her and declined the job.

When I returned to our apartment, Ann was on the telephone and said Sears wanted to talk to me. It was the Assistant Store Manager. He said he had talked with both the manager of the store in Richmond and Newport News. He said that he felt he could hire me as the part-time assistant manager of the paint and electrical department if I could work each evening from 5:00 to 9:00. I assured him I could, but asked what kind of pay he was thinking about. He said, "We have never paid a part time person this much, so you have to promise you will not tell anyone what you make." I went to work and was always treated extremely well. They even gave me two weeks' vacation with pay.

There were several part-time people who came in at six each evening. Les Hill, the manager of the two departments, had been with the company a long time. He was delighted to have me there and soon stopped working any evenings himself. We met briefly each day, and he told me what had to be done. They sold a lot of paint and in a busy evening, one person had to stock the shelves. The salespeople did not like to do this because they lost some commissions.

One of my jobs was to close the register each evening and take the cash and credit card receipts to the cashier, salesman, who was a full-time employee, but not the sharpest person I have ever known. If there was an error, he had made it. If there was a problem with a customer, his personality often made it worse. One evening he approached a lady and asked if he could help her. She responded, "Don't get smart with me, young man."

When I reported to work one evening, Les said, "Ray, I have something to tell you, but I think you better sit down first. The salesman is resigning and entering the ministry." My response was, "Thank God he's a Methodist." He entered a small Methodist college and made the dean's list every semester. Years later, after we both had finished seminary, Les sent me an article that stated, "The salesman had been selected as the rural minister of the year for the state of Kentucky." God rarely calls the able but when He calls, if they respond, He enables them.

In my second year of seminary, Dr. Dale Moody returned from a sabbatical leave at Oxford after he had earned a second doctorate. He was absolutely the brightest of the brightest and had a photographic memory. He used a dialogue method of teaching. Class usually began with his asking a student a question. He often took the opposite position and encouraged the class to jump in. In no time he became my favorite teacher. His tests were always one question. He read the tests himself and they came back with red notes all over them challenging what you had written even if you had made an A. I once wrote an answer entitled, "seventeen reasons why Doctor Moody is wrong." He gave me an A+ and told me I had to do a doctorate in systematic theology with him.

The second year was more interesting and enjoyable than the first because I took a class with Dr. Moody each semester. Since he had convinced me to focus on systematic theology, I took courses with other professors in the theology department. Dr. Eric Russ's course in Faith and Reason was a course that forced me to think about the nature of faith and the bases of science and math. Later in life this enabled me to enter into dialogue with the college professors and students in two different congregations that I served.

By Thanksgiving, Ann was pregnant with our second child. We decided to go home for Thanksgiving week rather than Christmas. Two friends from our days in Richmond, rode with us. We were all talking with each other and didn't turn on the radio for the entire trip. We only stopped for gas and bathroom breaks. In those days most bathrooms at service stations were outside, so we never talked to anyone. When we arrived at Ann's mother's home, she told us that President Kennedy had been killed. As we watched the drama of the change of power in our country, the President's funeral, and the assassination of Lee Harvey Oswald, I remember thinking everything has changed. One man, if he is willing to give his own life, could change a country and the world.

When we left Louisville at Thanksgiving, there was a light snow on the ground. We did not see the ground again until late February. It was one of the coldest winters on record. For over a week the temperature was below zero. Every morning the men started their cars, so their wives could drive to work. One night we had a heavy snow and the temperature dropped to 20 below zero. As I went out, I noticed a neighbor with his car jacked up putting on chains. When he finished and got into his car, it would not start. My car did not start either. I wondered what kind of pastor he was going to be with such a lack of common sense.

Our finances were doing better with me having two jobs and Ann one. The seminary had doctors which we could see for free. The Kentucky Baptist Hospital also gave students a 50% discount. Some of my friends told the dean of students that I needed some help with the hospital bill for the delivery of our upcoming child. The dean called me in and said he had funds for student aid and gave me a letter stating that the hospital bill should be sent to him. Having a second child meant the cost of day care would not justify Ann working for the $200 per month she was making. She decided she would babysit to earn some money. I also added a full day Saturday to my schedule which meant I worked until nine every Saturday night and left to pastor the church early Sunday morning.

Ray Allen, Jr., was born on March 11, 1964, in the middle of a massive storm that covered the eastern United States. Because of the closure of so many airports, Kate, Ann's mother, flew for over 12 hours to get to Louisville the day he was born. It normally would have been a two-hour flight.

With a girl and a boy, I felt our family was complete. The church was ecstatic. For over 50 years, there had not been a son born to a pastor. The men tapped me on the shoulder and said, "You are a real man." The ladies gave a shower and gave more suits of male baby clothes than Ray, Jr., could have ever worn. One man, who had three daughters, asked me what I did to get a boy. He just knew there was a kind of secret his father had not told him.

Going on for a doctorate degree was still my goal, but in the first semester of my senior year, several things happened that put a damper on those plans. First, I had little time for anything but school and work. The only exercise I was getting was a game of golf at 6:00 on Monday mornings. The local course let students play for a dollar. Ernie Boyd, Harvey Skinner, and I began playing. All work and no play make Jack a tired, dull boy. Since we played no matter how cold it was and we were all young, we soon were shooting in the 80s.

Second, I stumbled academically. I had to complete more than a full load in the fall and spring semesters plus take a full load in summer school. During the middle year and senior year, I was in a clinical group with Dr. Wayne Oates which counted as field work. It was an excellent learning experience. I enrolled in a pastoral care course with him. He was out of town during the course's first week. During that week, his student teaching assistant taught the class. He made us write a lengthy evaluation of one of Dr. Oates's books. On that paper I made an A+. We also did a time study of the first week of class. The teaching assistant wrote on my study when he returned it that I did not have time to do justice to the course and I had to drop the class. I declined to do this until I could talk to Dr. Oates. When he returned, he told me that what the teaching assistant had said was wise, but he had reviewed my seminary record and I could continue.

The week just before the midterm, Ann's grandmother died. Mama Sally had been Ann's primary care giver after the death of her father. We went home for the week, and the day I returned to class, we took the midterm exam. Dr. Oates told me I could take it later. I chose to go ahead and take the exam—Big Mistake. His exam was the worst I have ever taken anywhere. At least half of the exam was identifying quotes from the reading or matching authors and their books from the footnotes in the assigned reading. The class did poorly and complained. I failed the test. He stuck to his guns and said we needed to know the literature in the field. He told me he wanted to see me in his office after class. I went expecting him to say I had to drop the class. Instead he offered to give me another test since I had missed the class the week before. I thought for a few minutes then told him I would not have studied what most of the test was about, so I felt it only fair that my grade remain. I earned A's for the rest of my work in the class. He gave me a B for the course, the only one in my senior year.

The third thing that happened was that Beth was getting ear infections at least twice a month. The doctors decided to pierce her eardrums and enlarge her eustation tube with radium. Even with the doctors not charging and the hospital giving us a 50% discount, it cost several hundred dollars. Ray,

Jr. was an allergic baby and couldn't keep any milk down. If you laid him down to sleep, he had great difficulty breathing. Ann and I spent many nights holding him so he could breathe. Finally, the doctors put him on a great deal of Benadryl and a meat-based formula. Both children improved. We were hardly keeping our heads above water physically, emotionally, or financially. During that year, Walter Johnson's Sunday school class sent us checks and Paul Crandall, the director of the Richmond Baptist Association, occasionally sent us a note saying he had prayers for us and included a small check. Even with their help, some weeks were too long for the money.

The fourth thing to happen I took as a sign from God. Each person wanting to enter the doctoral program was required to take the Miller Analogy Test. I have never figured out why. It is basically a cultural background test, and I surely was lacking in that category. The test is no longer required at any seminary that I am aware of. The score for entering the doctoral program had to be 50 or above. My score was 35, which meant I would have to complete a Master of Theology degree before entering the doctoral program. This added another year of courses and a short thesis. It became clear to me that I needed to go be what I had been called to be—a pastor.

Before class on the day after I received my score, I went to see Dr. Moody. I told him what had happened. He assured me that he could get me a conditional acceptance into his doctoral program. I assured him that I was fine with leaving the seminary and taking a church. He said he would go talk that day with the alumni secretary and encourage him to find me a church. I told him I was sorry I would not be able to continue to study with him. He gave me a fatherly hug and said, "I'll send you my reading assignments. You may not have the degree, but you can have the knowledge of the degree." I walked out of his office with a burden lifted from my shoulders.

As my completion of seminary approached, others were getting called to churches, but in late June, I still did not have a church. Grady Nutt graduated from seminary a year ahead of me. We had some classes together, but I did not know him well. Some readers will recognize him as one of the stars on the television program, *Heehaw* until his early death in a plane crash. Prior to that, he worked as Director of Alumni Affairs for the seminary. Grady saw me in the hall and asked me to stop by his office. He said Dr. Moody had asked him to find me a pastorate in a college church. He said Wise Baptist in Wise, Virginia, had contacted him looking for a pastor. I knew that Wise was in the coalfields of southwest Virginia. I did not know there was a college there. He told me that the first community college in Virginia was started there and that many of the teachers and students went to the

Wise Baptist Church and he felt it would be a good place for me to start. They had requested that he send someone for a weekend interview. I agreed to go the first weekend in August.

It seemed to take forever, driving the crooked roads of eastern Kentucky. We finally arrived in Pikeville and drove over the mountain to Wise. Wise is a beautiful mountain town of 3,000 people. It is the hometown of the late actor, George C. Scott and of Carroll Dale, the famous Green Bay Packers football player. The church put us up at the Wise Inn.

The chairman of the committee was Joe Smiddy, the director of Clinch Valley College, which was a branch of the University of Virginia located in Wise. He was out of town on college business during that weekend. I preached and Ann and I met with the deacons and other church leaders. We felt very comfortable with the people, and they were soon talking as if they were sure I would become their pastor. We drove back to Louisville and arrived late Sunday night. My only concern was not having met Dr. Smiddy. Monday evening he telephoned me and advised me the committee had voted unanimously to recommend me to the church if I was in agreement. To say the least, we were excited about the opportunity.

The next Sunday night he called back to say the church had voted to extend a call to me. The only problem he saw was the church had purchased a new parsonage and was in the process of remodeling it, and we would have to stay in the old parsonage for a week or two. The salary would be $4,800 per year, a house with all utilities included, a car allowance, and convention expenses. This was less than I was making at Sears without a degree. We worked it out that they would send the movers the first week of August, and we would begin on August 13th.

I finished my last class, but could not graduate until January since there was no summer graduation. We drove home to Amherst to spend a few days with our families. The funds we had were almost nonexistent so another loan was desperately needed. Kate went with me to her banker, and with pride reminded him of the first loan he had given me to go to seminary. She seemed pleased that we had made it through school, and for the first time, I felt she did not see me as her son-in-law, the loser. The banker loaned me $1,000 to buy some furniture and see us through until my first payday. I felt vindicated because it was one of the banks that would not loan me money to continue at Virginia Tech 10 years earlier.

REFLECTIONS ON SOUTHERN SEMINARY

I left seminary feeling I had received a first-rate theological education. It had been a tough academic journey. Some think seminary should be like church or Sunday school, but it is not. At the time I felt that there should have been more effort in teaching the student to become a leader of volunteers.

I had done well, but it had come at a high price for me and my family. If I were doing it again, I would have taken four years. I had to make an A in order to feel accepted. When someone does this to himself, he is on the ever-turning, never-ending wheel of the hamster cage. True self-acceptance is not based on grades, position, or money. It is that we know we have, through grace, become a child of God. Since God knew I had not come to that place yet and was a fatherless child, he put a good father figure into my life, Dr. Dale Moody.

WISE

On August 13, 1965, we began our ministry as the pastor and pastor's wife of the Wise Baptist Church in Wise, Virginia. Wise, at that time, had a population of 3,000 plus. It is the county seat of Wise County. The leaders of the county and of the coal industry lived there. A few years earlier, the University of Virginia started the state's first community college (Clinch Valley College) in the county poor farm. The United Mine Workers also built the Appalachian Regional Hospital in the town. Several physicians lived in the town. The church attendance usually numbered around 100 people. The congregation was better-educated and more affluent than any other church in the county. It was truly a great place for an inexperienced young minister to begin.

My first Saturday in town I decided play golf. I took the mismatched clubs that my father-in-law had given me and went to the Dan Hall Country Club. It was a beautiful place on top of a mountain. The course was very busy and the pro said that he had a threesome ready to tee off and it would be best if I played with them. He introduced me to the group. It was obvious that they did not look forward to dragging the new preacher along with them, but after I birdied the first hole—a short par four—and played the first nine at 41 and the back nine at 40, they really warmed up to me. Their best score was a 92. From then on, many townspeople wanted to play with me. Rumor was that some said Wise Baptist had called a preacher that even played golf.

Things went smoothly for the first month. Ann and I worked hard at getting to know the names and everything we could about the people. We were glad to be there, and they expressed their happiness at having us. The first Sunday in October, our first crisis occurred. The local association of Baptist churches met during that week. On Sunday morning a small group of women gathered around the pastor's study door. I invited them in, but only the wife of the wealthiest man in town came in. I left the door open. She made sure that I knew who she was and that they were the strongest givers in the church. She then told me that the director of missions for the association was an embarrassment to Baptists and should be fired. She more or less ordered me to go to the meeting and move that he be fired. I thought, "I can't possibly do this, and if I did, she would be my boss from now on." Calling her by name I replied, "What you say may well be true, but I do not even know this person. I am the newest pastor in the association, so I cannot and will not do this." She said, "Then I will stop giving to the church and to your salary." Trying very hard not to lose my temper, I softly said, "That is your choice, but I still will not do it." She marched to her Sunday school class with the other ladies following her. I went home and told my wife that we may be out of a job by the end of the month. I expected her to come to the monthly business meeting and have me fired.

The next morning before I sat down in the office, the church phone rang. It was John, the lady's husband. He asked, "What did Ida say to you yesterday?" I told him. He then asked, "What did you say?" I told him. Then the shocker, "You did well. You will not have any more trouble out of her. See you Sunday, Preacher, and I will be sure to put my monthly offering in."

He did. Thursday morning he called me and asked me to play golf with him that afternoon. I am sure the ladies made sure everyone knew what had happened. Nothing else about it was ever mentioned to me, but by way of feedback, one of the deacons patted me on the shoulder and said, "I am glad we have a real man for our pastor."

God could not have chosen a better place for a young minister to start out than the Wise Baptist Church. Where I had grown up, it was the custom to call the pastor Mr. and his wife, Mrs. In less than two weeks, everyone was calling us both by our first names. They invited us into their homes for meals. They volunteered to babysit for us so we could have a night out. The Kiwanis Club invited me to become a member. The Garden Club invited Ann to join. New people started coming. College students soon made the church their church of choice. We started a college choir. At the state Baptist Student Convention, we sent more students than some of the larger colleges.

The mountain people have a tremendous capacity to love and accept others, and in a real sense they live by the words in the play, *Oklahoma,* "the men are men and the women are women." I focused my outreach on men. I believed if you reached the men, or boys in the case of college students, the women would come. At first the women were not sure about my spending more time with men than them, but when they saw the men coming to church, they accepted this as a good thing.

Non-Baptist men soon were inviting me to play golf or fish with them. Once, a pipe-smoking Methodist professor and I went fishing. He stood up in the boat and fell in the lake, pipe and all. When he came up with his pipe, I told him that he had now been baptized properly because I had said over him and his pipe while he was in the water "In the name of the Father, Son, and Holy Spirit." Further, I assured him that we would be glad to receive him into the church on Sunday. Laughing, he asked that I keep this private. I have until now. Since he is in Heaven, maybe he can read this on a heavenly eBook.

The first year was full of the normal things that pastors do. I went to the church office each morning and studied the theology and pastoral care books that Dr. Moody and Dr. Oates had sent me from the reading lists for their doctoral students. There was plenty of time for me to learn to preach well. The church people were very complimentary of my preaching. When people listen and encourage, a caring pastor works hard not to be a disappointment on any given Sunday.

Not having to spend my evenings working at Sears gave me time to spend with the family, talk with Ann, and play with the children. One day Beth asked her mother, "When will Daddy go back to Sears?" When her mother told her I was not going back, she was pleased. It was a good time for us.

Not having all my time filled up enabled me to spend casual time with the leaders of the town. Most mornings at ten o'clock the court took a break. The courthouse officials and the men of the town met at the Coffee Cup. Often I took my break there, too. Soon the police officers, the clerks, and the commonwealth's attorney became friends. If one listens to the leaders, they will seek his advice. A pastor can effect change if he invests the time in caring for those who often serve in thankless jobs. Sometimes over coffee, I could not help but think I was living in Mayberry.

One morning I was having coffee with a Sheriff's Deputy. The town drunk, well-intoxicated, came in and asked him for a cup of coffee. The Deputy Sheriff gave him the coffee and said, "After you finish your coffee, go over and tell the jailer to lock you up." He finished and staggered off. A few minutes later he was back and asked, "what must I tell them to lock me up for?"

Good things happened there. The best con man in the town was a ten-year-old boy named Sam (not his real name). Sam lived with his mother on the back of a strip mine in a tarpaper shack. Most summer days he spent at the entrance to the swimming pool. He would have two dimes in his hand and with a pitiful look on his face would say, "If I had nickel, I could go swimming too." The mothers bringing their children to the pool knew he did not even have a bathing suit. He often made a couple dollars in a day.

Revivals were popular events during the sixties. The Methodist Church had a lay revival. Several scientists from Oak Ridge were the speakers. Sam heard about the services and figured this was a new group to con. On Friday night at the invitation, he was the first to respond. With tears flowing freely, he spoke loud enough for all to hear. "I am hungry because all I have had to eat all day was a small bowl of tomato gravy, but I am happy because I have been saved." After the benediction, the speakers took him to the Inn and they bought him the Inn's most expensive meal. On Saturday they bought him new clothes and a bicycle. After the Sunday evening services, they went back to Oak Ridge.

Within an hour of their departure, Sam broke into the church and stole the offering. He was arrested in the church parking lot. On Monday morning, Judge Bandy sent deputy to tell me the judge wanted to see me in his office. When I arrived, the Methodist Minister, was already there. They told me what had happened. The judge stated he did not want to send Sam to the reform school because of the bad situation he lived in, but he had to do something. He sought our advice. The Methodist

Minister suggested that if the judge would release him into his custody, he would take him to the Methodist children's home and attempt to get them to take him. The judge agreed if the church did not press charges. They took Sam. I do not know how Sam turned out. I have read the papers. I thought he might end up the president of General Motors or a leader in the mafia, maybe a politician.

Until the interstate highways were built, the area was isolated. The coming of cable television also opened up the towns to the world. Yet in the deep hollows of the area, to even hear a radio, one had to have a long outside antenna. As a result of this, some of the customs and words were unique to the area. On one of my first visits, a lady kept saying her husband went away. I asked, "When is he coming back?" With tears, she said, "He's dead." So much for being sensitive. It took a while to understand that when a person was referred to as "funny turned," it was not a reference to the shape of his body, but his mind. He was not crazy, but a bit strange. "He lost his courage" was not referring to no longer being brave, but meant he could no long function in the bedroom. "Asking to be restored" meant they were in a religious struggle and needed the joy of religion to return. Some referred to themselves as the P.I.E. crowd. Poor, but often they were far from poor. Ignorant, but often they were very wise, but had little formal education. Emotional, meaning they hadn't truly worshipped unless they felt strong emotion. Sometimes it meant they liked loud, emotional preaching. A frequent visitor said to me as she exited through the church door, "I told my husband—you can't preach a lick, but I can understand every word you say and it all makes sense."

The people were absolutely wonderful and they treated us as if we were members of their family. If someone died, they expected me to help them pick out a casket. They spoiled our children with goodies and gifts. The first Christmas, I believe every member of the church brought Ann, me, and the children gifts. My best gift was given by a poor lady who bought five pencils, sharpened them by hand, and gave them with a note saying she knew I had to write a lot. Soon they were all a part of our extended family. Harry Bird Dickinson, who became one of my favorite people, spent hours in his shop making Ray, Jr. a child's desk. Ray, Jr. became devoted to Harry. He would tell the barber he wanted his hair cut like Harry's. From then on, we saw our church members as family.

They knew how to love and accept a pastor, warts and all. Indeed their love often humbled me. There was a very quiet nurse in the church. I noticed her husband never came, but I was too busy to ask why. He died. Then I learned he had been badly injured in the Korean War. I did his funeral. After everything was over, she brought me a check for a thousand dollars as her tithe on his GI insurance. She felt very low when she gave me a note stating I was to decide how the church would spend the money. She helped me learn to notice the quiet, faithful people that are often neglected in every church.

In the first year I learned how to do funerals. In seminary I was taught that funerals were to be conducted in a formal, stately manner with a lot of scripture reading. The pastors' manuals of the time would often have an outline of a service that was all scripture reading with the advice that it was best to stick with scripture only. Some of my members had grown up in the Free Will Baptist Church. When their parents died, I went with them to the funeral. Often the pastors had not finished high school, but they did very meaningful services for the people. And they frequently lasted a couple hours and featured three or four preachers.

Almost always, they spent some time criticizing educated preachers who had choirs with robes. At first I took silent offense at their attack on me, but I soon saw that there was some validity in what they said. All of them told warm stories about the departed loved one, sometimes funny stories that filled the church with laughter, while others in tears told of their own grief and expressed deep hope for the afterlife. Their funerals were a celebration of life and the hope Christians have. When understood, their funerals helped the family. My funerals bored people. I changed, and worked at making them not generic but a celebration of the life of the person and the hope we have in Christ.

Although the people were extremely good to us, like all churches, there were enough negative thinkers and worry-warts to keep the work interesting. They often expressed their displeasure when the church did nontraditional ministries. One of the focus areas of the LBJ poverty program was southern Appalachia. The local Presbyterian minister resigned his church to direct the efforts for Wise County. There was a need particularly for the kids from the hollows to have some formal education prior to entering school. The school system wanted a head start program but could not raise the matching funds required by the federal government. The county ministers, including the Catholic priests and nuns joined together to recruit college students from all over the country to work in the program. The federal officials agreed that their volunteer labor would count as matching funds.

Each college student was paid $150 for the experience. They lived in Sunday school rooms and cooked their meals in the church kitchen. At the time, we were not using the four upstairs bedrooms of our parsonage. There were three bedrooms downstairs. Five girls stayed upstairs in the parsonage.

Ann and I wisely took the church dishes and stored them. The ladies of the church had a lengthy meeting with discussion over the great risk to which we were exposing their treasured dishes. A delegation was sent to advise me that the group could not use their dishes. I listened and told them Ann and I had stored them. They checked to be sure we had not missed any.

Most of the volunteers came from religious colleges and universities. Most were upper middle class and had no experience with poor people. They assumed all of the Appalachian people were poor and uneducated. They were surprised that all of the ministers had master's degrees. One volunteer leader, who was an Episcopal clergyman, while looking at the books in my study, asked if I had read all of the books. He was surprised to see a Baptist that had been to a theological seminary and read more of the great theologians than he had.

The volunteers assumed that to be poor meant you were unhappy. Most of the kids were underprivileged, but happy. Many of the children lived in homes that only used Anglo-Saxon (often four-letter) words, particularly for bodily functions. The pastors met with the volunteers at least once a week to help them better understand what they were experiencing. One worker shared with me that the children needed to learn some culture. A little boy had told her he needed to take a piss. I asked, "Is that really any different from saying, 'I have to pee'?" Another shared that she had told the children the story of *Little Red Riding Hood*. When she got to the part about the wolf eating grandma, one little boy commented, "That dirty son of a bitch." They came to help and teach, but by the end of the summer they had learned and received significantly more from the people than they had given. Every one of them headed home crying.

One of the most remarkable citizens of the area was Joe Smiddy, the director of Clinch Valley College. He was chairman of the committee that called me to the church, a Sunday school teacher, and a deacon. The first director of the college did not get along well with the local people. When he resigned, the president of the University of Virginia looked for someone with experience in education who was established in the area. He lured Joe from a successful oil business to take the job. Joe and his wife, Rosebud, moved to Wise and lived on the county poor farm. There they guided the school from a community college to a four-year degree-granting branch of the university. This happened with strong opposition from many in the Virginia General Assembly in Richmond. The committee recommended that the college remain in the newly-created community college system, but the late Delegate Orby Candrill, the representative from Pound, Virginia, introduced a floor amendment stipulating that CVC remain a branch of the University of Virginia. The amendment passed. The community was ecstatic.

Joe was a gifted mountain musician with a storehouse of mountain tunes and songs. In a year when the state government was experiencing hard times and slashing the budgets of all the state colleges in Virginia, the Committee on Colleges came to Wise to investigate Clinch Valley's request for funds. He put the committee up in the best rooms the Wise Inn had, fed them a delicious supper, and invited them to his home for dessert and some mountain music. Joe, I am sure, provided them something a little stronger than coffee. They all had a foot-tapping good time when Joe and his friends played the ballads of the mountains. At breakfast the next morning, the committee informed Joe they were going to recommend that his request for the full funding of Clinch Valley College be approved.

It was later shared with me by another college president that one of the committee members remarked as they drove out of town, "Do you think we should drive through the campus, so we can at least say, if asked, that we saw the college?" Joe was a master of convincing people to invest in the school.

No student was every turned away due to lack of funds for college. As a last resort, Joe would telephone a coal operator who may or may not have finished high school and talk him into donating the fees for the student. Joe transformed the county poor farm into a fully-accredited branch of the University of Virginia. Clinch Valley College is the only state college in far western Virginia. Its graduates include a former Virginia attorney general and many college professors. Now thousands call CVC their alma mater.

Since the school was growing rapidly, several of the church members thought there should be a Baptist student center near the campus. A piece of land at the entrance of the college became available. The church agreed to purchase the land, but there were no funds. Harry Byrd Dickinson (who only attended college a week in his life) and I were commissioned to raise the money. We traveled and visited any Baptist who had two nickels to rub together and asked for one of their nickels. At the end of thirty days, we had all but $1,500 to close the deal. There was a wealthy Baptist in St. Paul, who was famous for his thriftiness. After over an hour, we convinced him to give $500. We knew that Paul, the wealthiest member in our church, was very competitive with the man in St. Paul. We called on Paul that afternoon. He hemmed and hawed about how hard times were and how he was not making as much money as he used to make and then took out his checkbook and asked, "How much did M.M. (the nickname of our St. Paul donor) give?" We gave an honest answer. As he handed me the check for $1500, he said, "Tight, isn't he? The next time you see him, tell him what I gave and ask him for more." Two lessons learned. You cannot get people to give unless you ask, and rich people often love to compete with each other.

Soon Harry approached me with the idea that we should buy a mobile home and put it on the lot. This would provide a place for the students to meet and hang out as well as provide an office for the B.S.U. director once we hired one. The trailer was frowned upon by our Baptist brethren in the East, but was very acceptable for the time being in that area. We headed out again with our hats in hand to visit our generous friends in Southwest Virginia. Again, we were successful.

The local mobile home dealer agreed to sell us a 12 foot wide model at cost. Since it was illegal to tow them on the highway and the state police had ticketed him every time he moved one, Harry agreed he would pay the fine. When we left, I told Harry I would help pay the fine. He said, "What fine? Let's go see Henry." Henry was Judge Bandy, the county judge, who was also a member of the Baptist church in Norton and had given Harry $100 toward the purchase of the trailer.

In the judge's chambers, Harry asked him to speak to the state police and tell them not to give the man a ticket when he moved our trailer. The judge said, "Harry, that would be against the law but I will pay the fine." As expected, an officer wrote the ticket as the trailer arrived. When the case came up, Judge Bandy had forgotten he had agreed to pay the fine and gave a long lecture about how this ignoring of the law had to stop. Finally the clerk of the court, Dick Sykes, one of my good members, got the judge's attention and asked to see him in chambers due to an emergency. In chambers, he was reminded that whatever the fine was it would be his. Judge Bandy also had a reputation for being tight with a dollar. He returned to court and said, "On second thought, I am going to give you one more chance. I fine you $5 and waive the court costs." The Lord does His work in a wondrous variety of ways.

Sometime later, Harry and Joe brought up over coffee that we should ask Virginia Baptist to hire a BSU minister now. I telephoned the department of student ministry and shared our request with the director, Bill Jenkins, who had grown up in the area. He told me he would be in the area soon and would like to meet with me and the associational missions director. He came and looked at our site and assured us that what we had accomplished was great, but there was no money in his budget and we would have to wait our turn.

This was shared with Joe, who had extensive expertise at appealing directly to the legislators when the state bureaucrats turned down his requests. He suggested I go to the next General Board meeting (the decision-making body for Virginia Baptist) and make my request personally. I went. The committee put a chair in the hall for me to wait until they were ready to hear me. After my presentation, the department head immediately stated that there was no money in his budget, and that this was not in his overall plan. To the surprise of everyone, Dr. Frank Voight, the director of the Sunday school department stated that he had enough money left over in his budget to fund the salary for a year, and he thought it was a great idea. I was excused and informed that the committee had approved my request without a dissenting vote. I went home on cloud nine. Later in the fall, the local association elected me their representative to the board, and a year later I was chairman of the committee that, a year and a half earlier, had placed the chair in the hall for me to wait to speak to them.

The Virginia Baptist General Board hired a campus minister for Clinch Valley College and the soon-to-be Powell River Community College at Big Stone Gap. The campus minister was a kind, caring person and became very popular with the students. Joe Smiddy, Harry Byrd Dickinson, and I were having coffee in the school cafeteria. Joe and I were praising the young minister's skills. Harry interrupted us with, "He will never make it as a minister." In mild disbelief, Joe and I responded, "Harry, what on earth do you mean?" His response, "You have to have a mean streak to be a minister, and he does not have a mean bone in his body." He clarified that every kind minister he had ever seen had been run over by the congregation and their kindness did them in as a leader. A year after I left Wise, campus minister resigned and returned to school to become a counselor.

There are always shadows waiting to jump out and kick you. Inside, one never gets over the significant losses as a child of abuse. Just a few days before writing this, I was receiving physical therapy in a professional office. The therapist, knowing I was a minister, shared how her father had deserted the family when she was small and that this was the greatest loss of her very successful life. I responded, "Your father was the one who suffered the loss. He did not get to be with his wonderful daughter. I would be very proud to have a daughter like you." She cried. Modern medicine can repair a physical hole in the heart, but an emotional one may never heal.

On the way home from a Baptist board meeting, I stopped at my mother's house for a brief visit. She had recently married Bill Stein, a man no one knew much about. My brother, Kenneth had a heating pad on his back. Supposedly he had hurt himself playing football. I thought it strange but said nothing. By now my brother, Robert was in the army and my brother, Edward was in college. Later they shared with me that Bill Stein had beaten them. As sad as it is, often an abused woman will choose another abuser.

A few weeks later, I received a telephone call from Roxie Ann, my married sister, that my mother had sworn out a warrant to have my three brothers, who were still at home, committed to a reform school as incorrigibles. The hearing would be in a week. My brothers, sisters, and I discussed the horrible situation and decided we would oppose her. The plan was to ask the judge, since Kenneth was a senior in high school, to let Roxie Ann and Bettie Sue, my other married sister, take care of him and let us be responsible for putting the two younger boys, Henry and Joe, in a private school. I went to court to speak on behalf of my brothers. To my embarrassment, my father-in-law and I had played golf with the judge hearing the case. The judge decided in our favor, but added that her children were not to go to our mother's home until she wrote a letter inviting them. All the others received a letter in due time; I never did. Sometime later, Bill Stein robbed the business where he was employed and fled. After he was captured, the police ran his fingerprints and it was discovered that he was an escaped convict.

We placed Henry and Joe in the Oak Hill Academy, a Baptist boarding high school in rural Mouth of Wilson, Virginia. I had gotten to know the president, Bob Isner, through my service on the Virginia Baptist board. He gave us some scholarship help and they seemed to do well. Henry made the baseball team, but there is always another shoe waiting to drop. At the end of the year, they ran away and were picked up by a local sheriff's deputy who brought them to my house.

What a dilemma. Could I take them into our home? I knew this would affect my family and my ministry at the church. Dr. Russell Schram was a physician who attended our church. He came to my study. Without inquiring as to the nature of the problem, he strongly advised me not to keep my brothers in my home. He correctly stated that it would be a difficult situation that would affect my children and my ministry.

I took his advice and contacted the Baptist Children's Home in Salem. Franklin Hough, the president, was very understanding of my situation. I am sure he and other leaders of the denomination knew what had happened, but were kind enough to never mention it to me. In the fall of 1969 at 31 years old, I was elected first vice-president of the Virginia Baptist General Association.

The church continued to grow and we added a fellowship hall and new office space. Many of the new members were college professors. They were all very supportive of me and my preaching. Dean Frank Stealy attempted unsuccessfully to have some of my sermons published. The Religious Herald, our Baptist newspaper, did publish a sermon (The Eye of the Beholder), which I preached at the local association.

The community continued to ask us to lead in community organizations. At the time, the Vietnam War was raging. The Red Cross asked me to be chairman for the county. One thing that was needed was someone to provide service to military families. This primarily involved verifying an emergency in a serviceman's family and talking to the Red Cross or the military to secure a leave for the serviceman. My wife, Ann, took over this responsibility. They installed their phone in our house which we located on top of the refrigerator. This kept the little fingers of our children from playing with it. It had a different ring from the other phone in the house. Beth, our older daughter, loved to yell, "It's the Red Cross phone!" This brought the war right into our home. Fortunately, not all of the calls were bad; some were about the birth of children, or that an injured son was going to be fine. Ann was good at it and never took "no" from the military. One day, she was bouncing youngest Katie on her shoulder while talking to a base commander. He asked, "Is that a baby I hear in the background?" When my wife confirmed that it was and that the baby was only three days old, he asked, "What in the hell are you doing at work?" Her reply, "I am not at work. I am a volunteer, and I am in my kitchen."

It was rewarding work, and it was also a way to repay the organization that helped me years ago when I was in the army.

In those days, particularly in small towns like Wise, ministers were invited to serve the community in numerous ways. I served on the advisory board for the hospital, and one of our tasks was to approve or withdraw a physician's privilege to practice at our hospital. Approval was routine and there had never been a case when privileges had been revoked. A physician became acutely mentally ill and was being treated by the local psychiatrist. The doctor had an argument with the administrator and refused to sign charts for more than 50 of his patients. The board revoked his privileges with the condition that as soon as he brought his charts up to date, he would be welcomed back to the hospital. He refused. Kenneth Asbury, the commonwealth's attorney for the court, was chairman of the board. The physician was a Baptist, so the board asked the two of us to talk with him. We did, but the doctor was hostile.

That night at midnight, the physician called and sang hymns. Through hysterical sobbing, he shared how his saintly mother had been a pillar in the church. She would turn over in her grave if she knew a Baptist pastor was trying to get him fired. Then he said, "I have a gun and will be there within thirty minutes to shoot you." I telephoned his psychiatrist who contacted the local police. The police and the commonwealth's attorney encouraged me to sign a warrant to have him arrested. I insisted that he was mentally ill and needed further treatment. The psychiatrist supported my position. Meanwhile, the officers had been dispatched to his house. He and his car were not there.

The next morning an officer took my daughter to school, another shadowed me as I went about my work. The doctor was not to be found. At midmorning, he showed up at his psychiatrist's office crying and asked to be hospitalized because he had done a terrible thing threatening to kill me when he knew I was trying to help. He got treatment, and I made the motion to restore his privileges. Such is the dull and uneventful life of a pastor.

On April 30, 1967, we welcomed our third child into the world, Kathleen Johnson Allen. It was a Sunday morning, and I asked Herb Tuck, the director of missions for the Wise Baptist Association, to fill in for me. The church marquee said, "It's a girl." When the associational newsletter came out, her picture was on the front page. When Beth and Ray, Jr., were born, I had been so busy that I had little time to enjoy them. One day, while Katie was crawling around my feet as I ate lunch, it dawned on me how much I cared for her. I realized that this must be the way God cares for each of us. He taught us not to address him as (the formal) "Father" but as "Daddy." In the Lord's Prayer, Jesus says, "Abba" which the King James Bible translates as "father," but the better translation is "daddy."

Prior to Katie's birth, I had performed the marriage of a physician (with a serious alcohol problem) and a lady bartender. His pastor refused to do the wedding. After the wedding, both the bride and groom quit drinking and returned to church. As an infant, Katie was hospitalized with lung issues and high fever several times. Each time, this physician cared for her and would never take any payment. Twenty years later, he was still sober and still married. One of life's great mysteries is who we fall in love with and what enables people to stay married and find healing. I have married couples who had everything going for them and their marriages failed. Others who had nothing going for them have lasted for decades. There is a chemistry that exists between some couples that no one else can understand.

Since our family had grown to five, vacations in hotels were too expensive for us to stay more than a couple of nights. We bought a big tent from Sears. With Katie still in diapers, a three-year-old, and an eight-year-old, we went to Sandbridge Beach, a few miles south of Virginia Beach. There the water goes under the sand and comes out several hundred feet from the ocean. With it came all kinds of small fish and sea life. We all had a grand week swimming and catching the critters.

The next summer we took a trip to Cape Hatteras. While we were there, the first astronauts landed on the moon. The East Coast was hit with hurricane Camille. When it started, we had gone to get groceries and the wind turned our tent over and scattered our stuff everywhere. The next spring we bought a new Camel fold-out trailer for $350. That sure made camping easier.

The response elicited from my older friends and neighbors to Neil Armstrong walking on the moon was very interesting. One was absolutely convinced that the hurricane was God punishing us for going where we had no business going. Another claimed it was a movie staged by the White House to get votes in the next election. In listening to them, both of whom liked to expound on their theories, I could not help but remember the words of an early Christian writer "Man's role is to think God's thoughts after him." Yet within the hearts of all of us, fear of the future leads us to deny the reality of the present and makes us want to go back to the past.

The University of Richmond opened a school of Christian education in Wise. They employed me as the part-time director and teacher. Even though the courses were religious in nature, they were accredited college courses. This allowed local teachers to take them and use them toward their certifications. Many did, and I enjoyed teaching the New Testament courses in particular. These also awakened my desire to further my education, but at the time, there was no way.

Even though we were a small town, we had wonderful mental health services through the Wise Regional Mental Health Center. They were fully-staffed with a psychiatrist, a clinical psychologist and a social worker. One had had a cleft lip which had been repaired, another had a hearing aid, and the other, a glass eye. They did excellent work, but the ministers referred to them as the "see no evil, hear no evil, speak no evil" crowd. This is not politically correct but it reflects the dark side of ministers' humor which they often can only share with each other. I conclude this portion with a salute to three of the best mental health workers I have every worked with: Drs. Nelson, Elder, and Ferguson.

In seminary, I had excellent training in counseling, so the center often referred people to me. At the time, electric shock treatment was sometimes given for depression. One case I was very familiar with was a farmer who came in almost monthly for a voluntary shock treatment. Then, without saying anything, he stopped coming. A staff member saw him in the grocery store and asked why he had not seen him lately.

His response was, "Oh, I give the treatments to myself now."
"How do you do that?" was the next question. The farmer
replied, "I bought an electric fence to keep my cows in. When
I feel a little depressed, I go out and lay my head on the fence
for as long as I can stand it. It works just as good as your
machine."

My observation is that every young man, once he has
learned his first job, begins to think of moving up the ladder
of success. Ministers are not immune to this ambition. In my
fifth year, two rather large churches came to hear me preach,
talked to me, but did not offer me a job because of my youth.
I was disappointed, but busied myself with working, fishing,
and golfing. I also became the volunteer golf coach at Clinch
Valley. It was great fun working with the students and going
to the matches at the college's expense.

In my experience, the best opportunities for me have come
at unexpected times and places. In Richmond, Dr. Polhil,
the retired executive director of the Virginia Baptist General
Board, became the interim pastor of Cosby Memorial Baptist
Church. I had attended college and seminary with his son,
John. Dr. Polhil had always been very supportive of me. He
telephoned and shared that he thought that I had good potential
as a leader in our denomination, but I needed experience
in a more typical Baptist church than Wise Baptist Church.
Cosby's pastor had been caught in an embarrassing situation
and left town in three days. He thought the primary job would
be rebuilding the image of the pastor. I agreed he could give
them my name. They extended a call to me; I accepted and
resigned as pastor at Wise.

The response of the church and community was surprising.
The church strongly asked me not to leave. Several members
came and said that my work had been a blessing to the

community and if it were a matter of money, they would contribute more to the church so that I could stay. The mental health clinic offered me a job as a pastoral counselor and offered to pay for me to become a licensed professional counselor. Since the family was very happy in Wise, sticking to my decision to leave was difficult. We left, but we left in tears.

REFLECTIONS ON WISE

First, I am forever grateful that I began my full-time ministry in the Wise Baptist Church. They laid the foundation for how I would live a life in the ministry. They created a loving environment that gave my children a positive attitude toward church and church people. All three of my children and their spouses are active in church and supportive of worldwide missions. They reach out to people, in large part I think, because they were loved by the whole town.

They taught me that minister is not a role you play, but it is who you are. That means a minister is not pretending to be a little Jesus, but instead is being who he is and letting the Spirit of Christ work through him and the people. They taught me that one did not have to be perfect or always right. When you acknowledge your missteps or poor judgments, people can forgive you and go on. From the church members and from my growing children, I began to learn that it was okay to play. Time spent with the men in the church and in the community built relationships that brought strong volunteers and funds to the church. It also made me a better human being and minister.

RICHMOND

On July 13, 1970, our wedding anniversary, we began our ministry at Cosby Memorial Baptist Church in Richmond, Virginia.

The church was larger than Wise, having over 800 members and a lovely campus with a building for each age group. I thought it was a promotion, but in many ways it was really a demotion. In Wise, our family had status. We were a big fish in a small pond. Here, we were a very small fish in a big pond. When a minister moves, he has to start all over, learning a new congregation and earning their trust so that he can lead. If he and his family were happy in the last place, they grieve the loss of friends, home, and surroundings. The children have to go to a new school. Shortly after she started school in Richmond, our oldest, Beth, asked if we could move back to Wise. I assured her that we would all like to do that, but we had to stay.

Within weeks of our arrival, the federal court ordered cross town busing of students to equally balance the races in the city schools. My children were not affected because we lived in Chesterfield County, but almost every family in the church lived in the city. The whole city was upset. I spent hours talking with families. Many days began at 7:00 in the morning and often did not end until 9 or 10 o'clock at night. Rumors of race riots in the schools abounded. While I was strongly committed to the integration of the schools, I did not see how busing a first-grader out of his community for 35 miles across town was the way to improve education. The Richmond police officers, black and white, were accused of being liars and racists. After talking with the police, I volunteered to visit the schools daily in our area of the city. Then, any parent could telephone our church and we would answer their questions with candor and honesty. One morning on the way to work, I witnessed two boys, one, African-American, the other, white in a fistfight. They were soon separated. By the time I got to my office, the media had a race riot in progress at the middle school. People telephoned the church, and we soon had stopped the rumor.

A few weeks later, a school bus filled with grade school students from the east end of Richmond turned over a few blocks from our church. The police came and took me to the scene of the accident. Fortunately, there were only minor injuries. Unfortunately, most of the children were poor blacks and their parents had to come across the city on city buses to get to their children. I talked with them and prayed with them. Their faces were covered with fear because they knew their children would have to make the long ride tomorrow. They cursed the judge who ordered this and of course, the judge's children went to private schools. The children and the poor are never consulted on what they want or need. These events greatly affected the four years I served the church.

We bought our first house, a small three bedroom rancher, in the Glen Conner subdivision of Chesterfield County. We were able to use my GI loan, so our payment including taxes was less than $170 per month. Nevertheless, things were more expensive than in Wise. So Ann got a job at Miller and Rhodes, a department store. She would have certainly preferred to stay home and care for the children. Soon, a church member helped her get a job at American Brands in the order processing department. This relieved the financial pressure we were under.

Judy Drake kept the children for us. She had a poodle that liked to jump up on people. One day while I was picking up Katie after work, they answered my knock with, "come on in." The poodle jumped up on my double knit slacks. I lightly slapped him on the head. He ran through the house barking and rubbing his head where I had slapped him. From then on, whenever he saw me, he started barking and rubbing his head. They would comment on how he never did that at any other time. I never told them why.

The first year I was there was a good year for the church. The deacons were aware of how busy I was working with the families upset over the busing. Since I had no time to visit prospects, the deacons volunteered to visit all of the church visitors. That year a record number of people joined the church. The percentage of visitors joining the church was at least twice what it was in Wise where I visited the prospects. It became clear to me that deacons and members visiting was a better way to reach out to visitors.

The church was primarily a church of young adults. We sponsored a fast pitch softball team, modified pitch softball team, and a basketball team. Most of them had played sports in high school, and we attracted many former college athletes. Many members attended the games, and high school cheerleaders and former cheerleaders often cheered. The fast pitch softball team won the city church league at least twice in my tenure. The basketball team only lost one game in four years. The church often made the sports pages of the paper. The church loved to play, but they were also good at ministering to each other.

Just before I became pastor, Vernon, a former college baseball player, had developed multiple sclerosis. Soon after, he was in bad shape. The men of the church learned to do his therapy. When I first met him, he was bedridden, yet he faced the daily degeneration of his life with faith and humor. His main contact with people was talking on the phone. He often shocked visitors by saying, "I have arranged for a phone to be installed in my casket, so I can call my friends from the grave." One Christmas he was in the hospital and very ill with a staph infection. The local television station asked if I would talk with the family about televising live his family opening their Christmas gifts from him, so he could see them. Most of Richmond watched. Since the television station had asked me to introduce the family, for several weeks after, children would come up to me and ask, "Are you Vernon's pastor?"

Vernon had been young, but he also had been a successful insurance salesman and had wisely taken out good health insurance and disability coverage. His family had the resources to meet their financial needs. Yet he saw the heavy toll this was taking on his wife and daughter. Shortly after I resigned to go to Blacksburg, he took all of his sleeping pills and never woke up. It was an honor to speak at his funeral. Most of the time when a person takes his own life, it is a defeated, selfish act; but in all honesty, I had to say that what he did, he did out of love for his family.

Apart from the social unrest in the city, it was fun to serve a church that had so many young people. In my first year as pastor, there was only one person on the deacon board who was over 55. Young adults meant there were also many children and teenagers. It also meant there was not a great interest in maintaining the church as an institution. When the church received funds from the sale of the parsonage, the young deacons, who as individuals usually spent all of their money as it was earned, wanted to spend the money on several projects they liked, such as more athletic equipment, improving the church kitchen, etc. After a lengthy discussion, George, the deacon in his sixties, prevailed upon them to appoint a committee to study what to do for a year.

Even though I was very close to most of the members in age, they expected me to plan and be at all church activities. I soon saw that if our growth was going to be maintained, we needed a second staff member who would work with youth and music. Since these parents were among the first "helicopter parents" who hovered over their children expecting and demanding the very best for them, it was easy to get the congregation to approve the position. We employed the Rev. Tom Mallory, who was in his early thirties and had one young son, Michael. It was an excellent choice.

Soon, Tom had developed a youth choir of 50 voices that sang at the Sunday night service. They were good and often received invitations to sing at other churches. When he began to use guitars and drums to accompany the group, some of the older members (who were few in number) mildly objected, but agreed that as long as we were reaching young people, it was a good thing to do. The high school boy he recruited to play the drums had not been coming to church but became very active. His mother, who was an excellent pianist, complained to me that she objected to drums in church. I was not very sympathetic of her view because I pointed out that drums had been used in worship long before the piano, and I felt she should be thankful her son was now in church.

Tom began a strong Thursday evening Bible study and recreation time for youth. The boys particularly loved to play basketball. The chairman of deacons was a dedicated man, but his wife was an emotional hothead. Their son, Pat and another boy got into a fistfight during a ballgame. Tom broke up the fight and Pat cursed him. Tom sent him home and told him he had to apologize before he could come back to youth group. His youth group was so popular that that was the only punishment he ever had to use. As soon as Tom got back to his home, Pat's mother telephoned and accused Tom of being prejudiced against Pat and told him to start packing because she was coming to the next meeting and making a motion to have him fired.

The next morning, Tom came into the office, told me the whole story, and asked me what I was going to do. My reply was that I did not take cussing from anybody and that if the church voted to fire him, I was going to quit on the spot. Nothing happened at the following week's business meeting. On Thursday afternoon of that week, Pat came to my office and stated he had come to apologize. I told him he was in the wrong office and that if he had been cussing me, we would both be apologizing because I would have slapped him upside the head. He then apologized to Tom and became one of Tom's strongest supporters. Later, Pat received a scholarship to play football at a small college. He also wrote me a note thanking Tom and me for making him face up to his temper problem.

As an aside, church staffs deal with this or get run over by people all the time. I hate to shatter the reader's view of the saintliness of clergy, but they know that someone is going to piss on every success they have. Sometimes, when a member of the clergy plans a big day, they try to guess at who will piss on the event. (Tom went on to have a great career, but unfortunately died of a heart attack in his early 50's.)

During my second year in Richmond, I was chairman of the Virginia Baptist Budget Committee. There was a disagreement with the administrator of the Baptist Homes which housed and cared for the elderly. I went to the home to discuss our position with the administrator. We finished our meeting at lunch time, and he asked me to have lunch with him in the resident dining hall. He introduced me to the residents, and after the meal a lady came to him and asked to meet with me. I talked with her in his office. I asked how I could assist her. She replied there were two problems with the home—"not enough whiskey and too damn much religion." I assured her I would take this up with the administrator.

In spite of all the turmoil, the church grew during the first year we were there. In almost every gathering of people, the conversation of busing was brought up. Those who could, sold their homes in the city and moved to Chesterfield County. This meant their children went to neighborhood schools. Some put their children in private schools. While there were racial overtones to both responses, their main concern was the safety of the children. Particularly in the elementary schools, the greatest danger was the long bus rides the children were forced to take to get to the school.

In the summer, some of the parents began to discuss starting a school, using our buildings. My feelings were split. I was for the integration of the schools, but my children were not being bused 30 to 40 miles per day. At first I was approached about the church running a school and my being the headmaster as well as pastor. I insisted that if the congregation supported a school in the buildings, it should be separate from the church. It should be run by a professional educator and open to anyone living in the neighborhood regardless of race. A retired school principal stepped forward, a board was formed, and the school received a charter from the state as "The Concerned Parents School." One of our members brought a motion to the church that they be allowed to use three of our buildings, and they would maintain those buildings and pay the heat and electric bill.

As moderator of the church, I announced the issue would be discussed in the next Wednesday night business meeting and the church would vote on a Sunday morning. In the meeting I said nothing because my feelings were split. Only one person spoke against the school and to their credit, they had small children being bused. The will of the people to have the school was obvious, but they wisely decided to have the vote two weeks later and to have a secret ballot.

The church was packed on the Sunday of the vote. I never told anyone, even my family, how I voted. I voted against having the school. My feelings were the law of the land—at least in the city of Richmond—was that children were going to be the front line of trying to solve the race problem. They were and still are used to try to solve America's ills. The church had voted and I, as the leader, had to try and make their decision work. The school opened in September of 1971 with approximately 300 children. No African-Americans applied. Some who had praised my earlier work to help the community by working with the schools and the police now called me a racist because they correctly felt that many of the people in the private school movement were prejudiced.

Virginia Baptist had employed Cesar Scott, a young, well-trained, and gifted African-American minister to work with college students. Without consulting anyone, I invited him to preach in our worship services. I told him I wanted him to preach his best evangelist sermon. I knew any true Baptist in his heart of hearts can never be against anyone preaching the Gospel. One member came to my office, and said, "I did not want his black behind sitting on a commode one of my sons might sit on." I told her that he would likely use the bathroom near the sanctuary, and that she was free to clean it after the service. She left the office somewhat upset. Caesar preached and hit a home run. His sermon was passionate for lost people and full of the spirit of Christ. When the issue came up in the next business meeting, the deacons encouraged me to invite him again.

Later, an African-American principal was assigned to the elementary school that my two youngest children attended. Ann and I invited him and his family to our house for supper. Katie, our younger daughter, had a good suntan from playing outside. She and the principal's daughter were playing dolls and his daughter asked if she was black. Later, he and his wife invited us to their home and we readily accepted. He was a fine man, loved the children, and was a far better principal than the white man before him. He remained in the school for a number of years.

Tom Mallory and I worked long hours to keep the attendance and giving from declining. We put thousands of miles on our cars visiting the hospitals. We often felt that we had 10 people in 15 different hospitals. The hospitals were located from one end of the city to the other. Soon we had worn out the cars we had when we took the jobs. I went to the Dodge dealer where the church secretary's husband, Rucker Barden, worked as a mechanic and bought a Dodge Colt station wagon. Tom, who was far more inclined to think everything through, read magazines and Consumer Reports and bought a Plymouth Cricket. His car had electrical problems and frequently would not start after a hard rain. One Sunday we had a hard rain during church and his car would not start. Rucker rolled up the sleeves of his white shirt and began to dry off the wires to the engine. As he worked, Tom commented he did not understand how this could be happening because Consumer Reports had clearly stated this was the best small car available. Rucker immediately replied, "I wish you would get that book to work on your car."

The situation in the community put a lot of stress on the families of the church. The minister's family is not excluded from the pressures of society and often, his having to deal with the problems of others leaves little time for his family or his own needs. The long hours were taking a toll on me. Ann having to work to keep our finances afloat meant the family had little time to play and be together. The third summer we were in Richmond, we took a week's camping trip to Seashore State Park. Since my schedule had not allowed time for reading, I took two books with me: Albert Ellis' *Guide to Rational Living* and Joe Karbo's *The Lazy Man's Way to Riches.*

I sat in the sand under a large oak tree and began to read. I thought that from Ellis' book, I would learn something that would help me counsel others and Karbo's book would be interesting. Soon I found myself engrossed in both books and reacting very personally to what I was reading. Their words forced me to enter a deep inner struggle.

As I read, it became clear to me that I loved being a minister, but at the moment was not very happy, in fact often feeling as if a doom were impending. Frequently I would dream that I had been drafted back into the Army, and they refused to let me be a chaplain. My life experience had taught me that even though I appeared to be successful, bad things were surely going to come my way. Inside, I blamed others or my past for any bad decisions I made.

As I read Ellis, he clearly and strongly made the point that whatever has happened to you in life, you decide what it means and how it is going to affect you. With a strong positive attitude, you could kill off the demons of the past. My strong background in the New Testament enabled me to see that this was in practical terms, the doctrine of Christian repentance. One could turn from a fear-ridden person to a person of faith. That a small amount of faith could in fact move mountains. Life will be whatever it will be, but we were free to choose our attitude and that would determine our altitude. The choice was mine. Before I finished, I had resolved that I was going to stop blaming or excusing and instead, begin to believe in order to see and then act in faith.

Still under the shade of my tree, I read the *Lazy Man's Way to Riches*. The heart of this book is that if we do not set goals in life, we drift. As I read, I saw clearly that most of what I had been taught about serving God was that one ought not set goals, but become passive and submit to what life brought. Then as I reflected on the *Bible*, most of the people God used—Moses, David, Peter and Paul—were far from passive. The rich ruler only came to do his father's will after he got to the end of his riches. So I decided to honestly put my goals and dreams before God and write them down, so I could read them and stay focused.

First, I really did want a doctoral degree, not just for the title but for the knowledge I would gain. As a child, I had read with excitement stories of people in other lands and I wanted to see the world. I honestly wanted to serve again in a college community. It became a lengthy list. Much of which was about the kind of person and minister I wanted to become. Each goal I wrote as if it would be achieved by a certain date. When we returned home, nothing I had written was a possibility anytime soon. I told no one about what I had done. The reason was, like Joseph in the *Bible*, family and friends often throw cold water on dreamers.

When I went back to work, I felt good; but I am sure no one noticed any difference in me. Richmond was an exciting place to be. One evening that fall I was in the middle of the Wednesday night Bible study when the police came in and interrupted the service. They asked me to step outside with them for a minute. I thought my family, who were at home at the time, had been in an accident. Instead, they said a man had climbed the channel six TV tower not far from the church. He was threatening to jump. Some bystanders had said he came to our church, and they wanted me to talk with him while two firemen climbed up and got him. I returned to the meeting, told them what I was going to do, and adjourned the meeting.

When we arrived at the television station, they had turned off the power to the station so that the man would not be electrocuted. A large crowd had gathered. Some were shouting, "Go ahead and jump!" They gave me a bullhorn. When I first spoke, he waved at me. The other two TV stations in the city had shown up and were broadcasting my talking to the man live. The firemen reached him and started down with him. The man's parents had arrived. The vice-president of the television station came to me and asked me to talk with the man's parents. He told me if they agreed to put him in a psychiatric hospital, the station would not press charges against him. I told his parents that if they agreed, the police would take their son to the mental hospital. His father blurted out, "I can't do that! People will think he's crazy!" I smiled and said, "Then, it's off to jail." At that point, they agreed to the mental hospital. The next morning the story took up most of the front page of *The Richmond Times*.

In the spring, we invited Dr. Dale Moody to come speak in the church one weekend. It was a great weekend for the church and our family. Mildred, his wife, came too. We also invited his daughter and her family. They lived about 70 miles away. We assumed they would come for a day. Dr. Moody insisted that they stay the night. Our house was less than 1,200 square feet, so there were children sleeping all over the floor, but it was a great time. While there, Dr. Moody told me Ann and I should go with him to Israel the last week of December. I told him we certainly did not have enough money to go. He shared with me that I could enlist church members and others to go, and that by gathering together a group, I would receive our trips free and maybe even some spending money. We signed on immediately. That was my first step toward seeing the world.

Things were going better for the family, and the leadership of the church was aware of how hard the staff was working. They recognized that with Ann working all week and my working every weekend, it was hard for our family to go anywhere, so they voted to give me an extra weekend off. On one of those weekends, we went to Cumberland State Park on a camping trip. I remember this because two things happened. I caught the largest bass I had ever caught at six pounds, and our younger daughter got lost. We were gathering firewood for a campfire; in our excitement we did not notice Katie had wandered off and it was getting dark. We began a frantic search for her but did not find her. When we returned to the camper, she was sitting on the steps. Her mother asked, "What happened?" She said, "I got lost. I was really scared so I sat down and thanked God for giving me a brain, then I figured out how to get back here."

Into every life rain does fall. One day, Ann was sick in bed and I was asking her how she felt when Ray, Jr. got home from school and asked to go play basketball in a nearby church parking lot. Later came the knock that every parent fears. A neighbor told me that Ray,Jr. had been hit by a car. When I got there, he was bleeding from the nose and mouth and was bruised badly. Ann and I went off to the hospital in the ambulance while a neighbor drove our car to the hospital. Fortunately, he was not hurt too badly and did not stay in the hospital. This upset me greatly. I wrote about this in my second book, *Our Common Faith.*

In the fall of 1972, I received a Master of Divinity Degree from Southern Seminary to replace the Bachelor of Divinity Degree I had received there in 1966. Information on the new Doctor of Ministries degree was also included. I immediately wrote a letter inquiring about the new degree and received a form letter outlining the grades I had to have and the tests I would have to take to be accepted into the program. Upon receiving the information, I wrote a letter to Southeastern Baptist Theological Seminary in Wake Forest, North Carolina. Dr. Ray Brown, my New Testament professor at Southern Seminary, was now dean there. He telephoned me and said I would be accepted and my grade point average was high enough that I would not have to take any of the entrance exams. Further, he wanted to meet with me and discuss a plan for me to obtain the degree. A few days later Ann and I drove to Wake Forest and met with him. He outlined a program where I would take an advanced clinical pastoral course at the Medical College of Virginia, take an individual New Testament research course, come to campus two summers and do a research project, write my paper, and then receive the degree. He agreed to supervise my doctoral work. One could not have a better supervisor than the dean of the school, but I also knew he was one of the hardest teachers I had ever had.

On December 27, 1973, Ann, I, and 16 church members flew out of New York for a trip to the Holy Land and Athens,

Greece. I cannot describe how excited we were as the KLM 747 lifted off the run way at JFK. One's first trip to the Holy Land is an unbelievable spiritual experience. In some ways, the *Bible* stories one has heard and read as a child are like fairy tales. But when one walks the Way of the Cross or drinks from Jacob's well, it becomes real. Since that first trip, I have gone to this remarkable place many times. I encourage the reader to go.

Shortly after returning from the trip, I began going to MCV every Wednesday for my class on counseling alcoholics and their families. Since I had a seminary degree, I was assigned—along with another Richmond pastor and a pastor from Germany—as chaplain to the alcohol abuse unit. Our trainer was a certified pastoral care trainer who was a Lutheran minister. We counseled patients in the morning and at least one of our sessions was videotaped. In the afternoon, the supervisor evaluated the session. The last hour of the day, we did group therapy with the patients.

Since we were ordained and fully-trained clergymen, each of us had to serve in the rotation as night duty chaplain. This meant that we had to stay in the on-call room where we could sleep until there was an emergency. One night when I was on call, I was called to the chaplain's office by the head nurse. The office was near the main entrance to the hospital. MCV was in a rough neighborhood. A prostitute had turned a trick in a car in front of the hospital and the "john" had not paid her. She was crying and asking for a chaplain. Basically, she wanted me to give her money to catch a bus to Fort Bragg where she said the soldiers gladly paid for her services. I refused to give her the money. She ran from the office into the lady's restroom saying she was going to take pills and commit suicide. I rushed to the head nurse to come and get her. She did. The prostitute then ran out into the street, and we never saw her again. The nurse thought that was one of the funniest things she had ever seen. Chaplain Allen was so inhibited he would not go into the lady's restroom to save somebody's life. She spread it among the nurses, and I never lived it down. In spite of this embarrassing moment, I completed the course with a grade of A.

In February, a member of the Blacksburg Baptist Church contacted me about recommending me to the pastor search committee of that church. A member of the Virginia Baptist staff also asked to submit my name. I told them both I was not interested, in part because the church was in decline, and the attendance and receipts were smaller than Cosby Church. I thought it would be wise to remain where I was until I finished my doctorate. Several committees of larger churches came to hear me preach but nothing materialized from their visits.

In April, Dr. Bruce Heilman, president of the University of Richmond at that time, invited Ann and me to his home for dinner. I had no idea what it was about, but we readily accepted. We thought other people would be there. To our surprise, there were no other quests. We were served a wonderful meal and afterward Dr. Heilman said, "The faculty of Richmond College has recommended to the board of trustees that you be awarded the honorary Doctor of Divinity degree and be invited to be the baccalaureate speaker." I was absolutely floored. I never dreamed that I would ever be recognized in that manner, let alone at 36 years old. After I took the babysitter home, I stopped my car and cried.

Earl Hamner, the creator of the television program, *The Waltons*, and a graduate of the university, was also awarded an honorary degree at the same time, but he was unable to attend the graduation. When Dr. Heilman introduced me for the baccalaureate address, he said, "In this graduation, we recognize the boys from the mountains of Virginia. Ray Allen is from Burly Hollow, Virginia. Every one of you knows exactly where that is. It is on the other side of Walton's Mountain." It was a great day. Governor Godwin also received an honorary degree at the same graduation. I really enjoyed introducing the governor to my mother-in-law. As the old saying goes, behind every successful man there is a great wife and a surprised mother-in-law.

The month of June, I spent at the Southeastern Seminary in a colloquium on Theology of Ministry. One of the teachers asked me why I was in the program when I had just received a degree from Richmond and few church people knew the difference between a D.D. and an academic doctorate. I was surprised at this but replied, "I hope to learn something." The new president, Dr. Randall Lolley, was living in the dormitory with us, and we all went out to supper together each evening. It was not only a learning experience but a fun time as well.

I went back to work renewed, but I also had to face at this time keeping the Cosby Church stable. It was a growing challenge because members with children were moving to Chesterfield County and joining neighborhood churches. On a Saturday evening in late July, I received a telephone call from Dr. Pat DeHart who identified himself as the chairman of the pastoral search committee of the Blacksburg Baptist Church. He said they planned to be in our service in the morning and would like for my wife and me to have lunch with them. I agreed. At lunch, they said they were very interested in me but planned to visit three other candidates. I was very noncommittal and expected to not hear back from them. I guess part of my hesitancy was my departure from Blacksburg years earlier, as it symbolized a difficult and sad time in my life.

Three weeks later on a Monday morning, Dr. DeHart called again. He said the committee had visited with the other candidates, and all the committee agreed they wanted me to become their pastor. Their goal was to have my first Sunday in the pulpit to be the third Sunday in September when the students would be back in school at Virginia Tech. I told him I was not sure I was interested in the job. He stated that it was obvious that I had not been to Blacksburg and seen how the town had grown. My reply was to ask why the church had declined and was now smaller than the church I was then serving. His response was that the church had great potential if it had strong pastoral leadership and the committee wanted me to see the town and church, and to meet with the lay leadership. He was very persistent and by the end of the conversation, I had agreed that Ann and I would come on Thursday to meet with them.

The committee had planned our visit well in meeting with the deacons and other church leaders. They showed us houses, the schools, and painted a glowing picture of living in Blacksburg. What impressed me most was the honesty of the group. I feared they were calling my resume, not who I really was. I knew the former pastor, and he was very passive, a trait no one ever accused me of. I pointed out that my style was to face issues head on. Dr. DeHart replied, "One of your references stated that Ray could be painfully blunt, and he thought that was what the church needed." I pointed out that the salary was a great deal less than I was making and that my present opportunities likely would lead me to much larger churches. Dr. DeHart responded that they knew the salary was inadequate and for me to write on a card what salary I wanted and needed. I wrote down a figure which was over one-third of what their previous year's receipts had been. He put it in his pocket and said that would be fine.

In our last meeting on Saturday morning, he said the committee wanted to recommend that I be called as pastor without the traditional trial sermon. I declined that suggestion and, to their surprise, insisted on a trail sermon and on meeting with the leaders of all the church organizations. Their response was, "Why?" I told them that I felt good about each of them, but I needed to get a feel for the congregation. The weekend was planned for the second following Sunday, after which they would have a business meeting to vote on me as their pastor.

Ann and I talked about the pros and cons of moving to Blacksburg. It would mean moving Beth, our older daughter, at the beginning of her senior year. It also meant I had to move in the middle of my degree program. It meant a larger salary, but a lot of hard work if the church was to be turned around after several years of dramatic decline. The list of negatives was as long as the positives. It was a major decision and the risk of failure was very high. Frankly, I did not know what I wanted or what I should do. Should I wait to be called to a position with a bigger church, or was I being called to do a job for God?

The entire family went to Blacksburg for the trial weekend. They put us up in the best hotel in town. It had an indoor swimming pool which the kids loved. There were no more than two hundred people in attendance. Other than the small attendance, the weekend went well. As we left, Dr. DeHart said he was confident that the congregation would extend a call to me but perhaps some would vote against it because of the salary. He asked if I would accept, and I told him that I was not sure what I would do.

On the drive home, Ann and I thought about the decision but did not discuss it with the children in the car. At home I told her I still was unsure. She assured me it was fine with her whatever I decided. The call came at about eight o'clock, which meant the meeting had been short. Dr. DeHart said 90 people had come to the business meeting, and all 90 had voted positively to call me. He said he had separated the salary question from the call vote and the vote on salary was 86 for and four against. He said the family that had voted no had discussed it with him, and he felt that their vote was because they did not make much money. I accepted their offer.

REFLECTIONS ON RICHMOND

The people of Cosby Memorial Baptist were fine, caring human beings. They loved God and often sacrificed their time and money to serve Him. Dr. Polhil was correct in saying they were a more typical Baptist church than Wise Baptist. Being their pastor was a learning experience for me. There, I came to see my talents and personality were better-suited to serve in a college environment. Because of my background, I thought the opposite—that I would do a better job and be more comfortable with working people.

There I learned that when leading volunteers, if you remained the leader, you could not always build sidewalks where you wanted them and expect the volunteers to walk on them. Instead, some needed to be built where the paths were. Then perhaps they would follow you down sidewalks that were not built on beaten paths. Examples of this were the private school issue and having Caesar Scott speak at church.

I learned that in the midst of social upheaval, the church could make a difference if, rather than being judgmental, it tried to serve and reconcile people to what was happening. We did help bring some peace to the parents in the school. The city police recognized this and appreciated our help.

There I saw that when the government uses schools as agents of social change by court order, the children pay a heavy price. Yet we continue on this path rather than being sure all our students can read, write, and balance a checkbook. I say this as one who strongly believes that every person needs the same opportunity to follow his dreams. The day the black church was bombed in Alabama, our daughter, Beth was walking to her Sunday school class hand-in-hand with her black friend. When our son started school, a relative asked him how many blacks were in his class. He replied nonchalantly, "I don't know because I never counted." Our younger daughter, Katie, was asked if she knew a black boy in her first grade class. She responded with a puzzled look on her face, "No one is black in my class." The woman questioned my wife as she knew there were black children in our children's classes. My wife explained to the woman, "Our kids don't think about skin color." When I went to Blacksburg, they had been politically correct on all of the social issues, yet there were no black members. When I went there preaching a simple gospel, several black families came and joined the church and became leaders in all areas of church life.

Finally, moving our older daughter at the beginning of her senior year was not a pleasant experience, but it all worked out well. In Blacksburg, she found her husband, Dean Cranwell.

BLACKSBURG

In late August of 1974, we moved to Blacksburg and I became the pastor of Blacksburg Baptist Church. Our first Sunday as pastor and family was to be September 13th. Even though Blacksburg Baptist was a smaller church than Cosby, we felt good about going. Ann and I were both convinced that this small mountain college town would be a good place to raise our family. Since the church was across the street from Virginia Tech, I thought it had great potential.

On the Wednesday before my first Sunday, I put my books in my new office; and when Beth, our older daughter, got out of school, I took her to the Leggett's store to buy a dress. While I was there, a hemorrhoid ruptured. Unaware of it until we returned home, I had bled through my suit trousers. I was admitted to the hospital. The surgeon recognized who I was and assured me I would be out in time to preach on Sunday, but I likely would have to have surgery the following week. I doubt I have ever been as embarrassed as I was then. My new secretary helped me see the humor of the thing when she told callers to the church office that I arrived and the bottom fell out. On Friday, there was more embarrassment. They flipped me upside-down and performed "the old stiff proctoscope." The nurse's aide rubbed my arm and urged me not to cry, but it was impossible to restrain the tears. Next they took me to x-ray for a barium enema. The surgeon and the radiologist got in an argument over whether I was bleeding too much to have the procedure. I stopped them by firmly saying, "Do it now or I'm leaving. It's my bottom you're discussing." Later in the day, the surgeon, a devout Catholic, came by and said God had removed the hemorrhoid perfectly, and I did not need surgery. However, I had to come back in six weeks for another proctoscope exam. I told him if I did, he would need a lot more help to hold me down. He laughed and discharged me from the hospital.

On Saturday, a dear, elderly lady came to our house and brought me a pack of stick-on sanitary napkins. She said if I used them and bled, no one would know. Thank God for thoughtful, little old ladies. This certainly was not the start in my new job I had envisioned, but God has a great sense of humor.

My first Sunday turned out to be a wonderful day. In prior years, most of the students had gone to other churches in town. To the surprise of most, they packed the place in order to see the new, young preacher. Fortunately, they came back the next Sunday and continued coming for the next twenty years.

I decided that for at least the first year, I would learn the people and the nature of the congregation. Many encouraged me to go hire another staff member immediately, but I resisted. Soon I began to see that the leadership was focused on not being the traditional Baptist church, and like most college churches were very much into appearing to be politically correct. Further, they did not have much confidence in the church achieving anything significant. Since their world was a thinking world, I decided my focus would be on doing the Gospel. On the first stationery, I added a little slogan, "The Church that's Doing Things."

Dick Howerton, the pastor before me, had been a better theologian than I and had a lot more sophistication. I decided that I had better stick to the Bible and apply it to the living of life rather than high-sounding ideas. I believed and still do that a Baptist has not been to church unless he feels something. As the congregation continued to grow in that first year, one member stated in my presence that he did not understand what was happening. When they had had a pastor who was a deep thinker, few people came to church. Now they had an educated country boy who told *Bible* stories and the place was packed. I am sure he wanted to say country bumpkin, but I took it as a compliment.

Through the years, the church had tried very hard to recruit African-Americans to become members, but none joined. In that first year, the T. J. Anderson family, (a wonderful African-American family) joined the church. Another member insisted that I have a meeting with some of the church leaders and form a committee to work on reaching more African-American families. In the meeting, Dr. T. J. Anderson said, "What black families want in a church is good biblical preaching, good music, and a good Sunday School for their children to learn the Bible." Since BBC already had those, he saw no need for the church to do anything differently to reach black people." The leadership took his advice. Several African-American families united with the church. Many served as leaders. Soon, on any Sunday morning, there were people from all races worshipping with us. When Tina Lee was asked by a student why she joined a white church, she replied, "I did not join a white church—I joined a church."

Since I was serving a rapidly-growing church, completing a demanding course in New Testament research, and working on my doctoral project, I was a busy fellow. I was researching how people grow spiritually and personally. There was a lot of testing of people and correlating survey results. Fortunately, my wife, Ann, was able to help me with this.

Shortly after Christmas, I took my second group of people to Israel. Our older daughter had not been a very happy camper with our moving during her senior year. So I took her with me as a co-host. A friend she had made in the church accompanied us. It was a great experience, but as is often the case when the cat's away, the mice will play. The church constitution made it clear that I would select all of the staff and recommend them to the church. I was away only ten days, but during that time, the part-time music director was transferred to another state and resigned. Since the music committee was accustomed to employing the music director and a member of the committee wanted the job, I returned to find that they had already hired a new music director. She was a very talented singer and had directing skills. I objected that the new constitution had been violated, which stated that the pastor would nominate all staff members. We reached a compromise wherein she would keep the job for a six-month trial period, after which, if I was not satisfied, I could seek whomever I wanted. I knew that this would not happen. If it did, I would have a church fight. Our option would only be a part-time person because of lack of funds. Things went well and she led the music program for six years.

In the spring, I began the search for a second staff member. I decided that the new person needed to be an experienced person who could work with college students and at the same time be able to do anything I was doing. Further, this person should, in personality, be very different from me, so that he would appeal to people that I was not appealing to. My only problem was that the finance committee could not see that the church could afford another well-paid person. Fortunately, Dr. Pat DeHart, the chairman of the committee that called me to Blacksburg, made an appointment to see me. Pat had also been Dean of Extension, the largest branch of Virginia Tech. In that role, he had hired many people, including Dr. Bill Lavery— later, the president of Virginia Tech—for his first job at the university. His visit was short but included some of the best advice I ever received. He

said, "Hire the smartest and most talented person you can find, but be sure he is loyal to you as leader. Then he will make you look even better. Pay him just a little less than you, then next year you will get a better raise. Don't listen to those who say we can't afford it because if you choose the right person, he will raise his salary the first year he is here." I took his advice.

Many people sent their resumes. The word of the turnaround at Blacksburg Baptist had spread, and many thought a growing university church would be the place for them. Little did they know that we were living Sunday to Sunday, and a time or two, I had to wait for my paycheck. I soon realized that Tom Reynolds was the best of the lot. He had a Master of Church Music from Southern Seminary and a Master of Divinity from Duke University. He certainly was as bright as I and his temperament and appearance were 180 degrees from mine. He was a few months older than I. As the dean's fellow, he had graded my music papers in seminary, but we had not been friends or kept up with each other after seminary. After many conversations, we both became convinced that we could work together. I was totally honest about the cash flow difficulties. His only request was to start a college choir, but not have anything else to do with music. The church, in spite of the concerns about money, hired him with a salary less than five thousand dollars per year lower than mine. We both got paid and true to Pat's statement, Tom's work brought in more than his salary.

Tom joined the staff in the summer of 1975 and got his feet wet immediately because I had to return to seminary for a month to complete my final doctoral course. After we moved, I had to change my doctoral research project. My first plan had been to work with a group of ministers using a case study method of improving their skills, but I knew that I did not have enough of a trust level with the local ministers for them to let me look over their shoulder. The committee agreed that I could work on personal and spiritual growth. To achieve this, I would have to develop a test that evaluated a person's level of maturity, recruit a group of adults and college students, and teach them the concepts that would assist them in their growth. To evaluate the project, I needed two control groups that would be tested at the beginning and end of the project. This would be done in the fall, and my paper would be completed and I would graduate in June of 1976. This meant I had a lot to do that fall.

That autumn was like a madhouse. When the students returned, they packed the church. Tom started the Blacksburg Student Chorale. The first Sunday they sang in church, they overflowed the choir loft. Everyone agreed a building committee needed to be appointed.

The owner of the local radio station, who had alternated the broadcast of Sunday morning worship services from church to church, approached me about having us do the program permanently. I took it to the church business meeting. The discussion was interesting. Some asked if I thought I was Jerry Falwell. I laughingly responded, "No, I am a lot better looking than he is, but I think that a church like ours should be on the radio." One member stated that we could not afford this and if we kept spending money like I was leading the church to do, we would soon be bankrupt. They voted to do it, but included that enough money would have to come in to pay for it, or we would stop after a year.

Tom and I took being on the radio seriously. We decided that we would do it right. He wrote a beautiful theme song, *Abundant Life in Jesus*. We called our time slot, "The Abundant Life Hour." He asked the director of band for the New Virginians, Paul Breske to compose the music. Later, I baptized Paul and his talented wife, Kathy. We agreed we would never ask for money. The response through the years was amazing. The chairman of the Republican party for the county was in the hospital with a serious heart attack. He had been listening and decided he should return to his Baptist roots. He requested he be allowed to join the next Sunday because he thought if he died he wanted to die a member. Charles Johnson survived and became a very dedicated deacon.

The cards and letters rolled in—often with checks in them. One Wednesday, we received a letter with $2.48 in it. It was a group of ladies in a nursing home who worshiped as a group with us and decided to take up an offering and send it in. One day, I was eating lunch alone in a restaurant and a man came over and asked if he could sit down. He said he really enjoyed my sermons. I did not ever remember seeing him before. So I asked where he sat in church? His reply, "Oh, I have never been to your church. I set my tee time at the country club for noon Sunday, drive to the country club, listen to the service, and tee off when you begin the last hymn." We received enough funds to pay for the first year. The Abundant Life Hour continued for all of my 21 years as pastor and after my time there as well.

At the first meeting of the building committee, they elected the chairman. I believe God picked the chairman. I did not know George Litton very well, but never have I worked with a wiser or more capable lay leader. He was a retired professor of animal science at Virginia Tech. The animal science building at Tech is named for him and another great BBC member, Paul Reaves. He was also chairman of the building committee for the large retirement community in Blacksburg, Warm Hearth. At the first meeting, it became clear that George planned to move forward and build a significant addition to the church. After this, one member resigned, stating that the problem with a good, small church was that a lot of people wanted to join it. Further, that member suggested that what we should do was plant another small church in the community, so everyone could know all of his fellow church members. The committee also decided that they should invite the chairman of a previous building committee who had developed plans for a building, but never built it, to join the committee so we could benefit from his experience.

Every experienced leader knows it is easier to lead a group of people to build a sidewalk where the paths are than to build a sidewalk where you want it and ask them to walk on it. Tom and I knew there was great sentiment to build additional Sunday school rooms. There was a widely-held but mistaken belief that churches grew through Sunday school, but at BBC, many came to worship, joined, and never attended Sunday school. Further, the staff could control the quality of the worship, but not the Sunday school experience. Our job, which proved not to be a small one, was to convince the committee and the church to expand the worship space first.

I started by taking George to lunch. I was unaware that he did not attend Sunday school. In a short time, he was convinced. It took a while to gently lead the committee to that position. One lady stated that all of the significant members came to Sunday school. She was an excellent teacher of a ladies' class. Later, when I wanted to start a second ladies' class for women, she resisted, claiming that all the ladies of that age were already in her class. I gave her a list of over 80 ladies who worshipped with us but did not come to Sunday school. Soon, the new class was flourishing. In the building committee meeting, she finally stated that she liked me very much and even though my position was not correct, she would support it.

The attendance continued to grow and donations increased. I was feeling pretty positive about things and, as is often the case with a pastor, a church member brought me back to reality. I was visiting the oldest member of the church, Mrs. Wall, in the hospital. She praised me for my excellent sermons and made several glowing remarks about my appearance, concluding with, "You are by far the best-looking preacher the church has ever had." I smiled and adjusted my bright red sport coat. As I left, she asked, "What color is your coat? I can't see anything—I am almost blind."

Easter Sunday was a five-star Sunday. On the Monday before Easter, we had a group of ladies hand-address a postcard to every single household in town. The message was, *"Next Sunday is Easter Sunday. If you do not have a church home, come worship with us at Blacksburg Baptist Church, 550 North Main St., 8:30 or 11:00 AM."* Over 800 people came. One of the groups in the church that wanted the church to remain small commented as he left church, "This is horrible; we had a bunch of strangers this morning." There is always in every church a group that thinks the church should exist to give them warm fuzzes. The good thing was that over 600 came back the next Sunday.

Shortly after Easter, the building committee shared with the church that their plan would be to expand the sanctuary into the fellowship hall, which would add 200 seats. This would increase the seating to 700. The expected cost would be $300,000. Then the fireworks started.

The member of the church wrote a letter to all of the church officers stating that I had given the church false financial statements and greatly overestimated the church's ability to afford any building program. He also claimed that the church secretary had forged some checks. Needless to say, this made me angry. The next morning, Ike Eller, a firm believer and gifted lay leader, came to my office with the letter. I quickly told Ike that if I had given out any false financial statements, the deacons should fire me. If the secretary had forged any checks, I would fire her. We went to see an attorney in the church. He suggested that the deacons should meet and that if the member could not produce any evidence of wrongdoing, he should make a statement that there had been a personality conflict between the member and the pastor.

In the meeting, the member could not produce a single check or document supporting his position. He became very angry that his judgment was being questioned, accused the chairman of deacons of being in my pocket, and therefore, could not see that I was going to bankrupt the church. Cooler heads prevailed and the deacons wrote a strongly-worded letter stating that there was no merit in the member's letter; and in fact, rather than acting irresponsibly, the pastor had acted wisely and professionally in this matter, and that the church plans for a building should proceed as planned. The following winter, the member slipped on an icy street and broke his tailbone. When the church office received word that he was in the hospital, Tom Reynolds offered to visit him. I thanked him and made the visit myself. It was and is my position that a pastor cares for every member of his flock. Though, I must confess that I would have loved to kick him in his behind at the end of the deacons' meeting.

This very unpleasant incident led me to see that just as my leadership was challenged in the army, it was being challenged here. I also knew that it was not over and would not be over until we were in the new building. Tom Reynolds and I stood shoulder-to-shoulder. He encouraged me by sharing that he had been studying King David, and that when David had to deal with someone, he did, and never slacked until they were defeated. As much as I would have liked to fight the way I did in the military, I felt the building expansion had to be done, and I had to refrain from taking any opposition personally. Those that opposed the expansion needed a graceful way out, and I was hopeful we could keep everyone playing on the team.

The building committee enlisted the L.L. Sams Company of Waco, Texas, to come and develop a plan to expand the sanctuary. The plan added the 200 seats and turned our worship space from a drab place with navy gray walls and black and white tile into a lovely, carpeted, well-lit space with the best sound system available at that time. Since Blacksburg is at 2000 feet elevation, usually the summer heat is not extreme, so we made the air conditioner mechanical-optional but included the duct work.

The business meeting was on a Sunday night and far from boring. The air conditioner was voted down very quickly. The next issue discussed was the committee recommendation that ten beautiful chandeliers should light the sanctuary. Hugh Duncan, a member of the building committee, had agreed to donate them in honor of his deceased wife. A member made a lengthy speech stating that they should be taken out and the money given to missions instead. Of course, the member was not giving his money for missions. I wanted very much to get up and call him what he was—a dumb ass. George Litton whispered to me, "Keep your seat. I will take care of this." He marked through chandeliers and wrote light fixtures. Then, he commented that if the brother does not want light chandeliers, we will have light fixtures. Nothing was changed but the words. Blacksburg Baptist has the most beautiful light fixtures I have ever seen. One member thanked the committee but stated that they had been misguided, since everyone knew you grew a church through the Sunday school. The heated discussion went on and finally the vote was called. It was 76 for and 72 against. The four passing votes were my family. I knew that the next day would not be pleasant.

I got to the office before our 9 o'clock opening time and Bob Mills was waiting there for me. I thought, "Now I'm going to hear it all over again." He had been the leader of "build the Sunday school addition first" group. I almost fainted when he said, "Ray, as far as my wife and I are concerned, the vote was unanimous last night. We do what we vote to do. My wife and I want to give the first gift toward the project." He handed me a check for $3,000. "I want to say one other thing. You are the best thing that has happened to this church since we have been members. We are proud to have you as our pastor." He became one of my dearest friends, and it was an honor to be called back after retirement to speak at his funeral.

The next two things to happen were not as nice. When Bob Mills left, two ladies who had made sure every church member knew about the treasurer's letter were waiting to see me. I asked them if it would be all right with them if Tom Reynolds joined us. I needed a witness to what I knew was coming.

They informed me that I had split their beloved church, and that I had no choice but to telephone that Texas company, tell them the deal was off, and announce what I had done to their beloved church on Sunday morning. I counted far past ten, pulled the church constitution from my desk, and read to them the statement that all decisions of the church would be by majority vote. Then, I very quietly stated that I did not have the authority to reverse the vote of the church, but that if they did, I would give them time during the Sunday worship to do so. Shocked, they said, "We can't do that! You sure better have those wall lights back on the walls when it's done. We made apple butter and sold it to pay for them!" They huffed out. On Wednesday, I received a note from one of their husbands. "Young man, you have gotten our church going again; do not listen to the naysayers."

The secretary told me the bank wanted me to telephone them. The president informed me that they were withdrawing the loan offer. I asked if there was anything that could be done to change his mind. He said the only way would be if there were written pledges for the first three years of the payment.

As soon as I was off the phone, Ike Eller came in. I told him what had happened. Like me, he has a little bit of a temper and said, "Let's go forward and find another bank." When we settled down, we decided to call a joint meeting of the deacons and the finance committee that evening. Ike shared with the committee what had happened. The committee voted unanimously to personally guarantee the first three years' payments. Every person endorsed the statement. I have never been prouder of a group of church leaders. I know that some of them had voted against the building program.

In June, I received my Doctor of Ministries degree from Southeastern Seminary. Since I had already received the

Doctor of Divinity degree from Richmond, our children began to refer to me as doctor squared. The graduate committee was very complimentary of my work and encouraged me to write a book. I am sure they wanted me to write a scholarly one. I had no interest in doing that and was far too busy to invest the time that writing a book required. I would never have gotten the degree finished without Ann's help from the beginning. Writing for me was difficult because my disability with spelling never went away.

The L.L. Sams Company began remodeling and expanding our sanctuary in June with assurances that we would be back in it before September 1st. The company proved to be extremely honest and very easy to work with. They were very sensitive to the people who wanted to keep the original pews and had the additional pews custom-made to match the old ones. They kept the lamps that the ladies supposedly made apple butter to pay for. They kept a memorial drape over the window and one used to cover the communion table. When we went back into the lovely, remodeled sanctuary, the lady who insisted on keeping the drape asked whose idea it was to keep that old thing up. Later, Velda Burkhart, one of Ann's best friends and a gifted lay leader in the church, gave a beautiful stained glass window to honor her husband and mother. In the window, a smiling Jesus stood with open arms welcoming the people to worship.

While the sanctuary was being enlarged, we worshipped in the theater that was half a block away. The theater put the sermon title on the marquee under the movie title. The movie of the week was *The Bad News Bears*. I do not recall the title of the sermon, but the following Sunday, the Roanoke Times featured a full page article on the church. This free publicity made all of their readers aware that the church was on the move.

The remodeling was finished on schedule, and we prepared to move back in. Many said that since we had 200 new seats, we should only have one service. Tom and I insisted that we continue with two services because this gave us space to grow. The first Sunday back, the early service had over one hundred in attendance and the eleven o'clock service was full.

I believed at that time and still do that a speech delivered with passion and conviction can motivate people. The congregation began to relax a little after we had been through the mother of all church conflicts and succeeded without losing a single member. Using this experience, Tom and I wrote an article for a professional journal on *The Management of Church Conflict*. Soon, we were doing conferences on the subject for clergy.

Not willing to let the enthusiasm wane, I preached a sermon entitled, *The Church on Main Street*. In it, I raised the issue that since we were located on Main Street across from the largest university in the state, we could not be just any Baptist church. We had to have not only a strong ministry here, but also around the world. That sermon stuck in the minds of many for years to come.

The building committee decided to delay the expansion of the Sunday school space until the remodeling was paid for. When they came to the October business meeting, they were prepared to resign and suggest that when the time came, a new committee should be appointed. The church rejected that idea and told the committee to go forward with the building. The committee asked our denominational experts on building and fundraising to come and give us advice. They came, studied our church, and advised us not to proceed with the plan because it was impossible. We thanked them, sent them back to Nashville, and went full speed ahead with the project. Since the former fellowship hall was now the back of the sanctuary, we had no space for church meals or parties. All of the wedding receptions had to be held in other places. We held the church Christmas party in the high school cafeteria. A crowd of over 400 came. During the evening, I invited all of them to the next year's Christmas party in the new fellowship hall at the Blacksburg Baptist Church. That brought cheers and a lengthy, standing round of applause. By the end of 1976, the plan for the new education building included Sunday school rooms, a fellowship hall, and an office suite that included a pastor's study and offices for three other ministerial staff members. The only discussion of the plan was about whether an elevator was needed. The committee had made the recommendation that our buildings be fully handicapped-accessible. Their position prevailed. I could not help but observe that one of the members who opposed the elevator later developed a health issue and had to use it to get to Sunday school class. The vote was 401 to 0.

The next question was, where would we get the money? The bank we had been using had created problems for us and we still owed them about $200,000. Some felt we had to continue to accept whatever terms they would give us. The finance committee, however, decided to seek bids for the money. I had moved my personal accounts to another local bank. We sought bids from both of the local banks and one statewide bank. We sent a letter to the three banks saying we would negotiate with the lowest bidder. Fortunately for me, because of weather, I was delayed in Europe returning from a Holy Land trip and was not present on the day the bids were opened. Tom Reynolds opened the bids and met with the finance committee.

All of the bids were for nine percent interest, but the bank we were currently dealing with had added a $2,500 set-up fee for the loan. This made First National Bank (the bank where I had moved my personal accounts) the low bidder. The finance committee voted to negotiate with First National Bank.

When I returned, Tom Reynolds told me what had happened. There was a note on my desk to call the president of the other local bank. When I did, he said he wanted to come by and negotiate the loan with me. I advised him that he was not the low bidder because of the $2,500 set-up fee. He said he had already removed that in order to keep the business. I told him that the finance committee had written that they would negotiate with the low bidder on the day the bids were opened, and that was what we were going to do. He told me that Bill Skelton was the chairman of the board of the bank and a member of my finance committee, and that he would go to the committee and have them reverse their vote. I patiently and quietly told him that as he well knew, I would do whatever the finance committee voted to do and told him goodbye.

Later in the morning, Bill Skelton telephoned me and asked me to go to lunch with him. I did not know him very well at the time, so I expected that he was going to carry the ball for the bank. At lunch, he asked me what had happened between Frank, the president of the bank, and me. I told him. He assured me that as a member of the finance committee he was for what was good for the church, and that I should continue as planned. I heard no more from that bank, and we placed the money at First National.

1978 became a full year. Dr. Ray Brown continued to encourage me to write a book on my doctoral research. He thought it should be a scholarly book. I got up an hour earlier every morning and began to write a book for the general public. I attempted to use only words a person with a tenth grade education would know. The work produced *How to Be a Christian, Happy and Successful.* I sent the manuscript to Boardman Press, our denominational publisher. They rejected it, saying that they had agreed to publish a similar book by another pastor. Skipworth Press, a new publisher, approached me about publishing the book. I agreed and the book sold over 5,000 copies in the first 18 months. Naturally, I received royalties from the book. The family had a meeting and said that since I had spent all of the extra money I had made from speaking at various events on the family, either I take the money and buy a bass boat, or they would. Naturally, I took their advice and also started going fishing on Mondays.

On August 2, 1978, at 3:00 a.m., my telephone rang. Since all of my children were fast asleep in their beds, I assumed a church member had had a crisis. A voice I did not recognize was on the phone. He told me that Richard Obenshain had been killed in a plane crash and requested that I tell his parents before they heard it on the news. Dick Obenshain had grown up in our church and was a candidate for the U.S. Senate. I spoke with someone I knew who was part of the campaign to be sure that this was not some kind of cruel prank. I telephoned his father's best friend to go with me to Sam and Jo Obenshain's home. When a pastor knocks on an elderly church member's home at 4:00 a.m., they know it's not a social call. Dr. Sam Obenshain's response was rather remarkable. When he opened the door, he said, "It's Dick! How bad is it?" My response was, "It's as bad as it gets." His reply, "What will Helen do?" His first thought was not for himself, but his daughter-in-law. After explaining to Sam and his wife, Jo, what had happened, I learned that Richard's children were visiting with them for the week. They asked me to tell his children. My wife came over and made breakfast while Sam and Jo made telephone calls and packed to go to Richmond. The children were comfortable with us because when the Obenshain children visited their grandparents, they often played with our children.

That day changed our state because John Warner took Richard's place and became a long-term member of the Senate. It also put me, a relatively unknown minister, before most of the leaders of our state. The family asked me to speak at the second funeral and burial, which was at the Mill Creek Baptist Church in Botetourt County. Several newspaper reporters telephoned me for comments about the family. The editor of the *Virginian Pilot* asked me for a copy of what I planned to say which he published word for word the morning after the funeral. Governor Dalton met with me to inquire what he might do for the family. Several of the national news programs closed the evening news with me making remarks at the head of the grave. Richard's son, Mark Obenshain, and my son, Ray, Jr., remain friends to this day. Mark is the Republican candidate for Attorney General as I write this, and our granddaughter, Katelyn, was a delegate for Obenshain at the Virginia State Republican Convention. Mark's sister, Kate, is often seen on the national news media commenting on politics.

On December 11, 1978, we dedicated our new educational building. It doubled our Sunday school space, included a fellowship hall that could feed 400 people, and created a new office suite. We concluded the day with our annual Christmas dinner, which overflowed the fellowship hall. Everything was great except that we wondered how we would repay over a half million dollars in debt, which the experts said we were not capable of doing.

In 1979, some good things happened to the family. In June, our older daughter, Ann Beth graduated from Radford University and was engaged to Dean Cranwell, a Blacksburg native and rising senior at Virginia Tech. My wife, Ann, who returned to Radford to complete her degree, graduated one quarter behind our daughter. We kept the promise we had made to Ann's mother many years before.

The year also brought a difficulty as well. In the summer, we went on vacation to New England. Our first major stop was Boston to see the Old North Church and a Red Sox game. We continued north to Dover Foxtrot and stayed most of the week on a farm with Ann's aunt and uncle. Our last stop was Bar Harbor, Maine. Arriving late in the afternoon, we checked into a motel, had lobster for dinner, and prepared for bed. Our son, Ray, Jr., complained that his ears were hurting very badly. I asked if he needed to see a doctor. He confirmed that he thought so. We took him to the emergency room of the hospital. The doctor diagnosed his problem as swimmer's ear and prescribed some medicine. We continued our trip, but his ears continued to hurt. As soon as we returned home, we took him to an ear, nose, and throat specialist. After he had diagnosed cholesteatomas behind each of Ray's eardrums, he referred us to Dr. McLean at the University of Virginia. A cholesteatoma is a tumor that destroys the bones in the inner ear. While in high school, Ray, Jr. had more than a dozen surgeries and at times, could not hear. Later, another doctor was able to replace the prosthesis with titanium, which lasts longer than the old types. He still has a hearing loss.

Having a seriously ill child is always a crisis. We had to deal with the uncertainty of whether or not the problem would be fixed. There was the demand financially of motels, food, and insurance co-pays. Parents have to make decisions concerning

treatments that will affect their children forever. Fortunately
for us, the schools understood and when he missed as much
as a fourth of the school days in a given year, they gave him
his assignments so that he could keep up-to-date. We decided
to not treat him as handicapped and let him have a part-time
job and earn his first car. He was on the school debate team.
He and his partner won the state championship even when his
partner had often had to tell him what their opponents had said
in order for Ray to hear. I am proud of how Ray, Jr. handled
this problem and still handles it well.

The last week of the year and the first week of 1980, our
entire family, including our future son-in-law, traveled to
Israel. It was a great family experience. We walked the Way of
the Cross and prayed together at the Stations of the Cross. On
day seven of our trip, we headed south to visit the Negev and
climbed Mt. Sinai. On this trip, Dean proved he could make
it with our somewhat adventurous family. On the way to Elat,
the bus had a flat tire. There was no jack. He figured out how
to change the tire with rocks. Early in the morning on the way
to climb Mt. Sinai, the spare tire rack fell off the bus. Dean
crawled under the bus and secured the rack. From that day to
this, if we face a difficult task, our family reminds each other
that we have climbed Mt. Sinai.

MURMURING

The church moved into 1980 with a spirit of optimism, but as is often the case when an organization has gone through a period of remarkable achievement, rather than rejoicing in the progress, a period of depression often follows. While the church had beautiful facilities, some began to find fault with the programs, and church music is often the place to find fault. Everyone is most comfortable singing the hymns they grew up with. During that year, I made a visit to the former church organist who was in her eighties. Naturally, she was aware of the "fussing," as she called it, over church music. She said, "Dr. Allen, don't you get discouraged over the church always fussing about music. I cannot say the church has fussed over music all of its existence because I have only been a member for 75 years."

Soon things had settled down and I decided to take a sabbatical leave. I attended a couple of conferences and spent a month as a visiting professor at Southeastern Seminary. I had over 90 students in my class and enjoyed very much sharing with the young ministers. The president asked me if I would be interested in becoming a seminary professor, but I assured him I was very happy at Blacksburg and planned to continue there.

In September, Dean and Beth were married in a church packed with family and friends. One year later they moved to Jackson, Mississippi, for Dean to go to law school. Thirty-three years later they remain married, and their two grown children, Michael and Rebecca have completed college, have good jobs, and are out on their own.

Fred Skaggs, a friend of mine, went to India on a mission trip and took some copies of *How to Be a Christian, Happy and Successful* and gave them to Indian pastors and students. In the fall of 1980, I began receiving letters from India inviting me to visit and speak to various Christian organizations. Since I had no interest in going there, I threw all of the letters in the trash and did not respond.

In September, I received a telephone call from Kunjamon Chacko. He had read my book and wanted to learn more about my understanding of Christianity. He invited me to come to India, to speak at crusades and at Bible College. I assured him I was not an evangelist, but a busy pastor and had no interest in going to India. His response was, "We need a pastor to come. A pastor loves people and does not care about the crowd. An evangelist loves the crowd, but does not care about the people." He said he would come to Blacksburg and we could talk further. I told him that was not convenient because my wife and I were leaving in the afternoon to go to a conference in New York. Before I hung up the phone, he had persuaded me to stop on the way in Richmond and talk with him. As we talked, he convinced me to at least pray about visiting India.

We were going to a conference of ministers at a camp in Pawling, New York. Norman Vincent Peale had invited a small group of ministers from all over the country and Canada to spend a week with him and Mrs. Peale. In the first session, he divided us into small prayer groups and said each of us were to share something with the group that was on our minds and pray together about it. I shared the invitation to India. It was a great group of men. After discussion and prayer, they all agreed I should go. I returned home.

Returning home several days later, over lunch, I shared with five businessmen from Blacksburg Baptist Church the invitation I had received from India. They confirmed I should not only go to India, but also go around the world, visit mission sites, return home, and share with the church what I had learned. Further, they would donate the money to finance the trip. The men in the meeting were Herb Alcorn, Bill Cranwell, Clinton Graves, Tom Hardie, and Bob Mills. I took their advice and headed to India. Years later, it was a great honor to speak at the funerals of the latter three.

AROUND THE WORLD IN 30 DAYS

On a cold January day, Bill Cranwell (who decided to accompany me on the trip) and I boarded the plane in Roanoke for Dulles International Airport. My feelings were mixed. I did not like being away from the family for an entire month, nor did I see myself as an evangelist or missionary. We landed in Bombay (now Mumbai) at 2:00 a.m. There were people sleeping in the airport and on the streets. One cannot describe the sights or the smells of Bombay in 1981. We taxied to the Centaur Hotel, where we tried to get some sleep, but our body clocks were eleven hours out of sync.

Later in the morning, we flew to Cochin. After arriving around noon, Kunjamon Chacko and his family met us and loaded us into a blue van and took us to Kottoyam, Kerala. We checked into the Aida Hotel, which was reminiscent of the forties in the U.S. Since we had five suitcases between us, Bill tipped the head room man five dollars, unaware that that equaled about half a month's pay for him. If we ordered coffee, Bill usually tipped the server a dollar. One of the room boys, and I say this because they were all in their teens, stayed by our door, eager to meet our needs.

Chacko had scheduled me to speak in a meeting an hour's ride from the hotel. Before the meeting, we went to a home for a light supper of rice with fish head curry. As I sat at the table trying politely to eat, I was acutely aware that jet lag had me feeling numb and the meal was in no way appealing to my American taste buds. My eyes were trying to focus on the house lizards that were trying to catch the bugs which were attracted to the lights. These critters are welcomed and ignored by the Indians.

Half asleep, I managed to get through my first sermon in India. My speaking partner was M.A. Thomas, the founder of the Emmanuel Bible College in Kota, India. He and his wife had walked over 800 miles to establish this ministry. He too was a remarkable man, a gifted minister and leader. He was a man of my size, and each evening, he wore the same suit. Before I left, he asked me to come to Kota to speak in his church and at the Bible College. I told him that if I returned, I would do that.

My host, Kunjamon Chacko is one of the most remarkable men I have ever known. At the age of 32, he resigned his job in business and entered the ministry. In 1981, he was working in prison ministry and with churches. His small salary came from Prison Fellowship International (Chuck Colson's organization). He and his family were living in a rented house with little money.

During our two weeks in India, I preached every night and spoke at several colleges. There was no television in South India at that time, so many people came. The services began with an hour of singing and then two preachers spoke for one hour each. A friend of mine spoke for only 30 minutes, and they asked him to repeat his sermon. It was not easy preaching longer sermons through an interpreter. To my surprise, several hundred responded by making a profession of faith in Christ.

The last two days, Chacko had me speaking at a crusade in the Kovolam Beach resort area. While there, we stayed in the Kovolam Ashok Hotel, a beautiful resort hotel overlooking the sea. The manager of the coffee shop was Gulpe. On our last day, Gulpe asked me to give him one of the red Bibles. It took me a moment to understand he wanted a copy of *How to be A Christian, Happy and Successful.* I gladly gave it to him. I share his story because it underlines how many Indians become Christians. The next time I returned to Kovolam, he said he had become a Christian and would like for me to come to his home for tea and meet his wife. As I entered his home, I observed he had hung a picture of Jesus beside the four other gods he displayed in his home. The second time I returned to India and his home, he had taken the other gods down and left only the picture of Jesus. The third time he had been baptized and joined a church. For most people of other religions, their conversion to Christianity is a process.

The two weeks flew by. At the end of our time there, Chacko pleaded with me to come back the following year. I agreed to pray and think about it. I assured him I was impressed with his work and dreams of ministry. Further, I shared that I was interested in establishing churches that would become independent and self-supporting.

Bill and I boarded Panama flight eight early in the morning and arrived in Bangkok, Thailand at 6:00 a.m. A missionary picked me up and took me to the mission guesthouse and Bill to a hotel. I was dead tired, but they were eager for me to see their work and kept me up all day and late into the evening. I was asleep the moment my head hit the pillow. While it was still dark, I heard someone singing. There was a knock on my door and I answered; standing there was a tall middle-aged man extending his hand. He said, "You must be Dr. Ray Allen. I am Steve Allen from Colorado. My job this morning is to get you some breakfast. When can you be ready to eat?" I replied, "Thirty minutes." We walked a couple blocks to a hotel.

Entering the hotel restaurant, it was apparent that everyone knew Steve. He and his wife were there as volunteers working as bookkeepers for mission work with refugees from Vietnam and Cambodia. Steve's order was, "my usual for me and my friend." Unbelievably, a plate of scrambled eggs, bacon, and grits was set before us: Southern cooking in Thailand.

After breakfast, Earle Gochart, a Southern Baptist missionary, took me several hours by car to his home, where we stayed the night. Earle was appointed by the Thai government to be in charge of refugee work for the country. His wife was a physician. The next morning, they took me to the largest refugee camp, which was five kilometers from the Cambodian border. A young Cambodian couple had crossed the border in the night. Early the next morning, she had given birth to a son. They were sleeping on U.S. army cots; their food was being provided by the U.N.; their nurse was a Dutch Reformed believer from Holland; and her doctor was a Texan supported by Baptists in the U.S. While we visited, the mother kept putting her hands together as if in prayer. I had often been greeted by Indians in this fashion, so I assumed she was simply greeting me. Dr. Gochart told me, "I think she wants you to pray for her son." With tears in my eyes, I took the baby wrapped only in a surplus army blanket and prayed for him and his family. I was reminded of another refugee child named Jesus. I felt proud that my country and fellow Christians were providing for this family in a tremulous time in their life, but also a blessed time in their life.

After five bittersweet, exhausting days in Thailand, we flew to Hong Kong. John and Ann Wong were two students sponsored at Tech by Elton Trueblood. John worked as our security person at BBC. Ann's father was a Baptist pastor in Hong Kong. He proved to be an excellent host both for the city itself and for the missionary work in this most modern city. He was very appreciative that my wife and I had been helpful to his children. I became aware that if I showed any interest in something I saw in a shop, one of his family would buy it and give it to me when we returned to the hotel. I knew they were not wealthy people, so I stopped looking at things. Since Hong Kong was and is a great place to shop, one afternoon Bill and I told them we needed to rest and went shopping alone.

Hong Kong in the eighties was a mission center for Baptists. There is an excellent seminary, a college, and a hospital there. It was a privilege to see the work being done and visit with the Christian leaders. By this time, I was genuinely missing my family. Changing time zones every few days was wearing me out. I decided to go home rather than spend time in Japan.

While in the Tokyo airport awaiting my flight, an interesting encounter occurred. While I was waiting there dressed in blue jeans and a flannel shirt, a soldier came up to me and asked, "Mister, can you explain this verse of scripture to me?" He had his finger on Matthew 5:32, the verse that makes divorce acceptable if one's spouse commits adultery. He explained that he had been overseas for two years and his wife had just had a baby. He was going home, but he did not know what to do. I soon learned that his wife was in Goldsboro, North Carolina. He asked me what I thought. I inquired if he still loved her. He said, "Yes, I do." The pastor of the First Baptist Church in Goldsboro and I had been in the doctoral program at Southeastern Theological Seminary together. I gave him the pastor's name, and he gratefully agreed to telephone him and arrange for counseling.

HOME

I arrived home happy to be back where I knew I belonged. The trip had been a great success. Yet, I was not sure that I was cut out to be a missionary. Like Jonah, I resisted the call to become involved in volunteer missions. Even though letters continued to arrive from Chacko emphasizing how much he and others had learned from my visit, I continued to struggle with split feelings about India and great happiness from my work in Blacksburg. The church continued to grow.

In the spring, the church voted to hire a full-time youth director. Tom Reynolds and I interviewed several students at Southeastern Seminary and Southern Seminary. We chose Bill Ross, a handsome former college basketball player. He began as assistant pastor for youth and education in late August.

His first day on the job, Bill came into my office with a question. "Where in the budget is there a figure for youth ministries?" Smiling, I replied, "There is no line item for youth ministry. Had we put, say, $5,000, that would have set a limit on what you could do. Since there is none, you can make it what you want it to be. By the way, you get to raise all the money, but I promise I will help." He left with a befuddled look on his face.

Soon it was obvious we had made a fine choice. Young people stuck to Bill like a magnet. He went to work as if there were no limits. Within the first year, he established a Fifth

Quarter program, which brought the Blacksburg High students to our fellowship hall for a movie and a pizza after football games. In order to show the movie, he raised the money to buy a big screen TV. We and a local beer joint were the first to have big screen televisions in Blacksburg. He also established an After Prom program. During the spring, he led the church to purchase a used van and a used bus in which he took the high school students on a mission trip to an Indian reservation in South Dakota.

As is often the case, staff members who are good at relating to others make those who are not as skilled stand out in a negative way. The youth choir program was declining while the college chorale that Tom Reynolds had established was booming and was the best college singing group in the state. After much internal struggle, I made the decision to relieve the music director of responsibility for the youth choir and asked Tom to direct the group. The number of young people singing in the youth choir increased dramatically. Several years later under Dr. Joe Borden's leadership, they were invited to sing at the Baptist World Alliance youth conference in Scotland.

Tom Reynolds and Bill Ross were absolutely two of the most outstanding ministers I have ever had the pleasure of working with. Their later achievements confirm this. Dr. Reynolds is now the retired senior pastor of the Harrisonburg Baptist Church Harrisonburg, Virginia, and Dr. Ross is the senior pastor of the First Baptist Church of Marietta, Georgia.

INDIA

In January of 1982, I traveled to India for the second time. This trip was very successful, but in other ways, a comedy of errors. Before Ann took me to the airport, a heavy fog had settled over the Roanoke valley and when we arrived, the airport was shut down. Dr. Joe Struther (my pastor when I entered the ministry) from Newport News, Virginia, was at the Norfolk airport and was going with me. I told him to go on, and that I would arrive a day late. Someone from Chacko's family would meet him at the airport, and he could explain what had happened. Joe checked his suitcase to go from Norfolk to Trivandrum, India, but instead, his luggage went all around the world on Panama flights.

Upon arriving in late evening, I was met at the airport by Joe and we boarded a train for Cunnor, India. At midnight, the train stopped and the conductor awakened us and said we needed to move from our compartment to another that slept four people. We went to the compartment and found it occupied by two Catholic nuns who were sound asleep. We told the conductor there were women in the compartment he had assigned. He replied, "That's all right. They can sleep on the bottom beds; you on the top." So our first night in India was spent sleeping above two Catholic nuns. We were awakened in the morning as they were saying their prayers. They thought nothing of being in a locked compartment with two American men. This happens all the time on Indian trains.

That evening, Joe and I spoke at a crusade in a four-room Catholic college and I slept in a farmhouse on thatched mats. I had to laugh when Joe undressed for bed, as his underwear was bright orange. We preached for several nights at the college and approximately 60 people were converted. With the new converts, we established the Cheropora Baptist Church and appointed a recent Bible School graduate as pastor.

On a later trip, I took a Virginia Tech graduate student in animal science. We traveled to Cheropora to dedicate their building, which Dr. Joe Straughan from Wise, Virginia had donated in honor of his mother. A Virginia Tech graduate student accompanying us discovered that the farmers let a calf nurse for eighteen months, thinking that they got more milk this way. He taught them to wean the calf and let the mother be bred every year, so that they would have a calf every year rather than two every three years. Two years later, one of the farmers brought his first-born calf from their newfound knowledge and put it in the offering at church. He called it his missionary calf. The student and his wife later became career missionaries.

Joe and I continued our journey from village to village speaking at crusades for four weeks. Our last stop was in Kota with a brief stop in New Delhi to talk with a group of Christians there. Due to flight schedules, we also had to stop in Madras overnight and complete our flight to New Delhi the next day. All of the hotel rooms were booked so we ended up in the bridal suite which was available because of a cancellation. The bed was a canopy bed decorated with fresh flowers. When I climbed into bed and looked up, I saw my reflection in a full-length mirror. I bemoaned to Joe, "The only time in my life

I will ever sleep in a bed like this and I have to sleep with a Baptist preacher."

We returned home feeling enthusiastic about our trip. I was confident that my missionary work in India was just beginning.

HOME AGAIN

The church was excited about what was being accomplished in India. The church was continuing to grow. I felt pretty good about myself—a poor boy from a mountain hollow who had been around the world. Further, we had established a church thousands of miles away. My first book *How to Be a Christian, Happy and Successful* had been a success, and Chacko had gotten permission to translate it into Malayam. Home, however, often has a way of bringing you back to reality. Sometimes at home, the realities of the past jump up and kick you in the shins.

It was late afternoon on a Friday when a teenage girl, whose family was active in our church, came to the office and asked to see me. She entered and it was obvious she had been beaten. In tears, she shared her story. Her father, a successful college professor well-known throughout our state, had beaten her mother; and when their daughter intervened, he had beaten her. I asked if it was the first time this had happened. She shared that it had happened before with her mother, but that it was the first time she had been beaten since she was small. I remembered seeing her mother at church with far too much makeup. I telephoned the parents and insisted that they both come to my office immediately.

When they arrived, the wife's face was bruised and she had a black eye. He immediately began to blame them for provoking him, knowing full well that he had a bad temper. They also deserved what they got because they did not show him proper respect as a husband and a father.

My inner reaction surprised me, because in a moment I was taken back to a night when I was 14 years old and my stepfather came home drunk and began to beat my mother. From my bed (which was over their bedroom), I heard him threaten to kill her. I jumped out of bed and ran down the stairs. He was holding a bed slat, which he had used to hit her. I stepped between them, stuck two of my fingers up his nose, gripped as tightly as I could, and pulled with all my might. He went down in tears, and blood went everywhere. I landed on top of him and gave him a beating that he would never forget. He didn't forget, because drunk or sober, he never hit me or my mother again. To this day, I am glad that I gave him that beating. At that moment, I was angry enough to give that professor the same kind of beating. At six foot two and 200 pounds, I could have done it with ease.

I gripped the arms of my chair and got my own temper under control. I knew that somehow I had to protect this teenage girl and stop her father's abuse. Very softly, I called him by name and said, "If this ever happens again, I am going to do three things: call the sheriff; report you to the social services department; and talk Virginia Tech President Lavery into firing you, which will likely mean that you will never teach again. The professor had first met me when I represented the University of Richmond at the installation ceremony for President Lavery. Further, I insisted that all of them begin counseling with a professional I recommended. I insisted that the two ladies swear they would call me if they were ever afraid again. I required that the professor shake my hand and swear he would never strike them again. The daughter later told me the beatings had stopped and thanked me for having the courage to lay down the law to her father.

This story is all true but disguised enough so no one can figure out who the people are. I share this to encourage those who have experienced abuse to seek help. Family abuse occurs in families from every level of education and success. It is a horrible plague. Around the world, many bear the shame of being the victims and some feel they provoked it or deserve it, but no child or adult deserves to be beaten. This event ended well. Most do not. If this is happening to you, *do not suffer in silence. It is not your fault. Get help. Otherwise it could end with you in your grave.*

It is often the case that with marriages, after about five to eight years, couples often begin to bicker and find fault with each other. This is also true of pastors and their relationships with their congregations. No one can ever live up to another's expectations. No church can be all that a pastor hoped for it to be, nor can he be all that the congregation expected. So in 1983, I became aware that there was a small group of people who were unhappy with me and with the direction the church was going. A deacon, who was also unhappy with me over several issues, brought up that people were telephoning him and suggesting that it was time that I move on. After a lengthy discussion, it was obvious that the deacon was the only one who felt that way. Nevertheless, I insisted that the church vote on whether I should continue or not.

At the business meeting to vote on my asking for a vote of confidence, the fellowship hall was packed. It was soon clear that they had not come to fire the pastor. After many affirming testimonies to my faithfulness to the people and vision for the church, the church voted without a single dissenting vote for the deacons to straighten out whatever the problem was, which was clearly not me.

During the meeting, the deacon, when confronted, admitted that only one person had telephoned him and complained. I felt there needed to be a way for the church to honestly give me both negative and positive feedback about my leadership. After a lengthy meeting, it was agreed that every year, each deacon would give a written evaluation of my work. Then the deacons' executive committee would give me a summary of their evaluations without any names attached. The church approved this and it worked. Each year, they gave me the evaluation which included areas I needed to improve and positive affirmation of my strengths. They decided to make it known that this had been done and that they added to each report that they were in full support of the pastor and his leadership. This continued until my retirement and contributed greatly to the harmony and success of the church.

Good things continued to happen in that year. Mary Wilson began English as a second language classes as one of our ministries. Hundreds of the wives and children of international students at Virginia Tech were taught English. During the Iran/Iraq war, students from both countries at Tech were in our classes. The mother of an Iranian student was in the school. Her husband, while on his way to Blacksburg, became stranded in Stuttgart, Germany. She came to me and asked me to write a letter requesting that he be given a visa to come visit her. I wrote the letter to the address of the embassy annex she gave me in Germany. The day that the letter was returned to me because there was no such address, she and her husband came to my office to thank me for getting him to Blacksburg. With their limited English, I could never get them to understand that I did nothing. It just happened.

That same fall, E. Y. Lau came and asked if he could begin a Bible study for Chinese students. He insisted that I speak to the group at least once a semester and baptize any converts. Many became believers and one year, I baptized 25 new mainland Chinese believers. The class later established a similar class at the University of Virginia and in Beijing.

Perhaps the biggest loss of 1983 to me personally, and to the church, was that Dr. Tom Reynolds resigned to become the senior pastor of the Harrisonburg Baptist Church. This is another university church in Virginia. He had a very successful ministry there and remained until retirement. He and Bill Ross had become very close friends. Together, we were a wonderful team of ministers and our time at Blacksburg Baptist Church was marked with creativity and successful ministry.

AN HISTORIC TRIP

In January 1984, I led a team to India. Dr. Bob Stockburger, a deacon at BBC, who was also my physician and friend, joined us and began a long, medical ministry in India. The nurse in his practice, Sue Altizer, and her husband, Terry, also went to assist with the clinics. Dr. Joe Straughan, a physician friend from Wise, Virginia, completed our team. Joe, on returning, gave the money to build our first church building in India, in honor of his mother. Dr. Don Reid, the pastor of Hillsville Baptist Church (and a friend and fishing buddy), was the other pastor on the team.

My work on this trip began in the city of Cochin where I spoke at a pastors' school sponsored by the pastors of the city. It was uneventful until the last day. Toward the end of school, I shared with them a time when, as a student at the University of Richmond, I saw on the library wall the pictures of the university's founders that were on display. I often looked at the pictures and wondered what these men were like. In my closing remarks, I said that I visualize in the future a Baptist school with a great library, and in it, pictures on the wall with names like Chacko, Thomas Sivadas, and the names of Baptist pastors who were present. They gave a standing ovation and for the next several years, I was always the last speaker at the pastors' conferences. Each time, they chanted, "Tell us the story."

I joined the other members of the team in Kottoyam. We were doing a medical clinic in a nearby village, where a Hindu man allowed us the use of his home for the clinic. Several hundred people showed up. One of them was Phillipos, a leader in the communist party. He asked me, "What are you doing here?" I replied, "We are holding a medical clinic." He inquired, "Why?" I said, "We are Christians and we want to help the people." We entered a lengthy conversation in which he shared that he was a communist and a leader in the communist party in the village. I invited him to come to the worship services which were being held in a rice paddy, and Don Reid was preaching. He came and brought his son and mother. His mother and son became believers at the meeting.

When his son grew up, he went to the India Baptist Theological Seminary and today is a Baptist pastor. In my many trips after this one, Phillipos came to many of the meetings at which I spoke. He began to tell people, "All of the other preachers who came from India said the people were going to hell and appeared they were glad to say this, but Dr. Ray Allen says, 'Life is tough, but with his friend, Jesus, you could make it.'" Recently, I received word that Phillipos is in regular attendance at a Baptist church but has not yet joined.

On the same trip in another village, I was speaking to a large gathering. A busload of communists showed up with lighted torches and began to march around our meeting. Chacko said there might be trouble and if there were, I would be the focus of it. He suggested I leave and he speak. Thinking only a minute, I replied, "I came to preach and I am going to preach." I was uneasy, to say the least, and at times, scared to death. At the end of the singing, I stepped to the microphone and preached on the resurrection of Christ. The communists continued to march. In my mind, there was an invisible line which they never crossed. At the invitation, over 50 people believed. The communists boarded their bus and never again protested at our meetings.

We returned home excited about how everything had gone. In two weeks, a shocking message came. The Hindu man who had loaned us his house to hold our clinic had been murdered by militants in the village. I still struggle with the question, 'Could a Hindu be a martyr for Christ?' I find some hope for him in the parable Jesus told of the two sons. One told his father he would not work in the vineyard, but changed his mind and worked. The other said he would work, but did not (Matt. 21: 28-31). Could it be that the story Andrew Greeley shares in one of his books is true? In it, Jesus complained to Peter that he was letting people into heaven that should be somewhere else. Peter's response was, "You will not like how they get in. I turn them away. They go to the back door and your mother lets them in." I do not know, but I hope Father Greeley is right.

I only remember one sentence from my seminary graduation ceremony. The speaker said, "Many of you will get your picture in the paper, but do not start posing for the picture now." For a month, I had been in India preaching and lecturing to people that hung on every word. I was really being treated like a celebrity. Home and one's normal work always treat you as average. In the mind of your wife, you are the same old husband she married; to the kids, you are just Daddy. Neither of them thinks what you say or do is particularly outstanding; it's just you. Where you work, they expect you to be and do what you have been doing, because that's what they pay you for.

In early 1984, we began our search for a full-time minister of music. We chose Joe Borden, who was a former army pilot.

He was completing his doctorate in church music. He joined our staff in June with all of his academic work completed, except his thesis. Joe was extremely talented; his major was music composition. Joe often wrote the Easter and Christmas musical programs. I felt that no one in our music program knew enough to challenge his musical knowledge. I also believed that as a former army captain, he had the leadership skills to deal with our people and move our music ministry forward. The only question I had was how a former officer would feel having a former junior NCO as his boss? That proved to be no problem. Veterans know someone has to be in charge. Joe did not disappoint me.

Early in his time with us, Joe produced musicals for Christmas that often attracted people from other churches to sing with our choirs. The excellent student chorale which had been founded by Tom Reynolds grew and often sang at statewide events. His youth choir was invited to sing at a Baptist World Alliance event in Scotland and also went on a European concert tour.

We also decided to add a third worship service. We did not attempt this to meet a space need but to provide different styles of worship. Bill Ross became the preacher at the 8:30 service which was patterned after the gospel tradition of most Baptist churches in the 50s. I preached at the 9:45 service, which was to be the new contemporary worship that was beginning to become popular. The 11 o'clock service remained a very formal service with me as preacher. What we had hoped would happen did not happen. Our vision was that we would reach a larger number of people. Bill Ross was one of the best young preachers I had ever heard. Yet the 8:30 service declined. Many of them began to go to the 9:45 service. A deacon called me aside one morning and said, "This congregation comes to hear the senior pastor. This is not going to work." He was right. When you have made a decision that is not working, the best action is to rescind it. So we went back to two services with me speaking at both.

We ended the year strong, with increased attendance and the budget fully-funded. The Hardie family also donated a piece of commercial property with the stipulation that it be sold and a retreat center built at Claytor Lake for all to enjoy.

A NEW DECADE

On September 14, 1984, I completed 10 years as the senior pastor of the Blacksburg Baptist Church. In that decade, I had put almost all of my time into the church, family, and India. Earlier in my ministry, I had been very involved in the Virginia Baptist General Association. I had continued to attend the annual meeting and occasionally attended the Southern Baptist Convention. The only exception to this was the five years I had served on the board of trustees of the University of Richmond.

Early in 1985, Bill Ross informed me that he felt he was ready to become a pastor and asked me to recommend him to a church. I did so, hating very much to see him go. He had developed probably the most successful youth program in the state. In the spring, he resigned to become the pastor of the First Baptist Church of Hillsville.

Meanwhile, the church paused to remember the past. The memorials committee decided to have a portrait painted of all the pastors. They were to be hung in the vestibule. These pictures became known as the *Wall of Witnesses*. Each one was dedicated as it was completed. My friend, George Litton spoke at the hanging of my portrait. My grandson, Michael unveiled the picture.

In the Baptist denomination, controversy was raging between those who felt that all the leaders and schools of the denomination should be required to hold the same views on scripture and theology, and those who, particularly in Virginia, were far more open to each person's freedom to express his faith as he felt led to, with no need to hold to a rigid ideology. I and most of my church members were in the more open camp. I had no desire to become a leader in this, but I did plan to attend the Southern Baptist Convention and vote for the more moderate candidate.

I was scheduled to fly out on Sunday afternoon. On Friday, Lucy Crawford died. The family asked me to speak at her funeral, but said they wanted to work with me on the schedule so that I could go to the meeting. The service was in the church on Sunday. Early Monday morning, I rode in the hearse with the funeral director to the graveside service in Greenville, South Carolina. He took me to the airport, and I flew to Dallas, arriving late in the evening. The next day, Winfrey Moore, the moderate candidate, was defeated by Charles Stanley. On impulse, I made my way to the platform, nominated him to be vice-president, made a strong plea that he be elected, and that he and the president work out the issues that divided us. Dr. Moore was elected. A firestorm started.

Ann and her stepfather were watching the evening news when, to their surprise, the screen filled with me and the closing statements of my nomination speech. I received a beautiful letter from Governor Baliles and hundreds of letters from others. The letters were overwhelmingly supportive, but some accused me of plotting the whole thing. Others called me a skunk and a wild liberal. Since we had recently acquired a computer, we answered every letter, even the ones that were not so nice.

In the next deacons' meeting, the chairman, encouraged the board to support my getting involved and pay my expenses for whatever travel was necessary. Several Virginia pastors telephoned me and suggested that I assist a group that was forming to support a more moderate president of the convention. I agreed and ended up having a meeting in Atlanta one month and Dallas the next month for the next two years. Our efforts proved unsuccessful. After the defeat of Dr. Dan Vestal for president of the Southern Baptist Convention, it became clear that the fundamentalists were in charge of our convention and were not going to let us in the more open group have any say in the denomination.

We decided the churches needed an alternative to the Southern Baptist Convention. The idea of a fellowship of churches that held to the ideals of our Baptist forefathers— soul freedom, freedom to interpret scripture without having to conform to a creed, and a missions program that included schools and medical care—was formulated. Dr. Ray Spence and I were asked to represent Virginia in this effort. Several of us maintained that we should become a new mission based on having most of the work done by volunteers. Since the majority was more inclined to provide funding to the missionaries that lost their jobs, this position won the day. When the leader of the foreign mission board was fired, he was employed to lead the Cooperative Fellowship's mission program. They do good things, but this approach failed to unleash the thousands of volunteers who: are gifted; would go almost anywhere in the world; would do everything a career missionary does, and in some cases, do it better.

It became clear to me that the fundamentalists' next effort would be to take over state conventions. At the end of my year on the steering committee, I chose not to continue but to devote my efforts to keeping the fundamentalists from taking over the Virginia Baptist General Association.

Meanwhile, back at the church, we did not have a youth minister, so I decided to take the youth on their summer mission trip. One beautiful Sunday afternoon, I and two vanloads of high school youth set out to repair homes in the eastern Kentucky mountains. This is really not a job for a middle-aged man. One of the projects was to build a room onto a mobile home for a disabled man. A third of the youth worked with me on the project. One was Jeremy Freeman. My memory says that he was a senior at the time. I had just purchased a new pickup which we took on the trip. The church's policy (which I wrote) prevented anyone under 25 from driving church vehicles. When we needed supplies from the hardware store, I asked Jeremy to take my truck and get them. I thought nothing of it. Later, I recommended Jeremy for a full scholarship to the University of Richmond, which he received. He went on to medical school. When he finished school, he joined my family doctor's practice. I was seeing my physician and Dr. Freeman heard my voice. He came into the examining room and said, "I will never forget what you did for me. You let me drive the first pickup I ever drove." It is truly amazing what impresses a teenager.

If one is happy and remains sane in the ministry, he or she must have a sense of humor. At 6:00 a.m. one morning, my phone rang. It was an elderly widow. She explained that she and her sister had been in a car wreck. Her sister had been killed, and she was in a neighboring hospital. She said that the doctor was ignoring what she wanted to do, so she wanted me to come and take her home immediately. This lady was one of the wealthiest ladies in our church and her sister was far from welfare. They never wasted any money on automobiles.

Both of their cars were over 20 years old. When I arrived, she was shouting, "Young man, if you do not discharge me now, I am going to call my lawyer as soon as he gets to his office and have you arrested for kidnapping." Her face lit up when I walked in and she said, "Dr. Allen, straighten out this young man and take me home." The doctor, with a frustrated look explained, "She was hurt in an old car and has no supplemental insurance. I was only trying to get her into a nursing home that would accept a charity case and she has been raising hell with me all morning." I explained that she could afford anything she wanted, and that I would take her off his hands and see that she got the care she needed. His response was, "You can have her, and good riddance."

On another occasion, I visited the home of a young couple whose wedding I had performed. The wife's grandmother had died. They were busy packing to leave and their new baby was fretting. I suggested that I rock the baby while they finish getting ready. She told me the baby probably needed to be burped. I succeeded in getting a burp loud enough to be heard in the front yard, cuddled the baby under my arm and rocked her to sleep. When they were ready to leave, I prayed with them and walked to my car. When I reached into my pocket to get the keys, the keys and my hand were covered in baby barf. Somehow their darling baby had spit up in my pocket. I had no handkerchief. The only way I could get my keys clean was to shake the barf off, which took awhile. I am sure that their neighbors thought the Baptist pastor was losing it.

During the time that all the troubles with Jim Baker were flooding the news and Jerry Falwell had taken over the PTL Club television program, an elderly lady in our church was waiting outside my office one day when I arrived. She came in and shared with me that she had always watched the PTL Club and that something had to be done. She said she had prayed about it and come to the conclusion that I was the only person who could straighten out the mess. Further, she said that she would hate to lose me, but that she had called Thomas Road Baptist Church. She was sure Dr. Falwell would call me before the day was out. So I needed to stay by the phone. I thanked her for her confidence in me. After she left, I telephoned her daughter and suggested that she check on her mother. The call from Dr. Falwell never came, and by Sunday, the lady had moved on to more important issues. Being a pastor is rarely boring.

Sometimes a pastor is criticized for off-handed remarks. On one occasion, I spoke at a conference at Virginia Tech about leading volunteers. Somewhere in the middle of my third session on how to lead volunteers, a minister asked what my theory of leading volunteers was. I must confess that my response was perhaps too much a reflection of how country I really am. I replied, "It's the cow-chip theory. You keep throwing your ideas against the wall and when the volunteers grab something and run with it, you have a volunteer program that has the support of the volunteers and then they will work." Everybody laughed. One of our newer members complained to a deacon that he was embarrassed that Dr. Allen would say such a thing. She replied, "You don't know Ray very well. I'm just glad he cleaned it up a little before he said it."

Being a pastor also means church emergencies often interfere with family events. In May of 1984, our son-in-law, Dean Cranwell, was scheduled to graduate from law school in Jackson, Mississippi, and our first grandchild was due. On May 9, 1984, I was visiting Frances DeHart, who was very close to death. Our plan was to leave immediately when advised that our daughter was in labor. One of the church secretaries paged me at the hospital and told me that our daughter had gone into labor. Mrs. DeHart died shortly thereafter. I certainly wanted to speak at her funeral since her husband, Pat, had been chairman of the committee that had called me to Blacksburg, and both were dear friends. That afternoon, I put my wife, Ann, on a plane and she headed to Jackson to welcome Michael Dean Cranwell, Jr., into the world. I arrived four days later. When our first granddaughter, Rebecca Allen Cranwell, was born, I was in the middle of a very important business meeting. Again, Grandma went to welcome her into the world. By now, our daughter and her husband were living in Roanoke. When I arrived, the nurses let me hold Rebecca. The date was July 12, 1987, one day before our wedding anniversary. Katelyn Hope Forbish, our third grandchild, and the daughter of our baby daughter, Katie, was more thoughtful of Granddaddy's schedule. She was born on May 20, 1994, and Ann and I were at the hospital for the labor and delivery. She has proven to continue to be very thoughtful of others. Shortly after she was born, I got to hold her. It is hard for me to describe the wonder of welcoming one's children and grandchildren into the world.

Early in 1986, Joe Borden and I began a search for a minister of youth and education. That combination was a very popular job at the time, but in a church like Blacksburg Baptist, it was an impossible job. Bill Ross had developed one of the most successful youth programs in the state and had devoted most of his time to youth. In choosing Gary Metcalf, we were going with a very different personality. Gary's strong talents were working with adults and his organizational skills.

He successfully developed a community food pantry that was manned five days a week. Its purpose was to provide aid for those with temporary financial difficulties. When Ann and I added a room on to our home, one of the carpenters asked to speak with me in private. He shared that during the winter, he had lost a lot of work and his daughter became ill. She was prescribed an expensive medicine. If they bought the medicine, there would not be any money for food. His wife came to the food pantry and received enough food for a week. He thanked me for what the church had done for his family. This ministry was soon supported by the entire community and continues to this day.

Perhaps this is as good a place as any to mention the support staff that worked with me during my years in Blacksburg. The support staff in any church is a valuable resource. Shortly after I became pastor, I insisted that they be provided the same benefits that the professional staff were provided. This was not the case in most churches at the time. Richard Caldwell was the custodian at the time and later, because of this policy, he was able to retire with a pension. Gail Taylor was the church secretary and bookkeeper when I arrived. She worked in many capacities until she resigned in 1994. Susan Cruise became our church secretary in 1981, shortly after she finished high school. Later, she became my Girl Friday. She continued on staff after my retirement. At Richard Caldwell's retirement in 1988, Sherman Wright became our custodian. He was so good at his job that I never had to be involved in the care and maintenance of our buildings. He became a good friend and continues as my friend to this day.

During the decade of the eighties, the church continued to grow. I continued to lead trips abroad through a travel agency and made more mission trips to India.

After I had been to India several times, I felt that things were developed enough in the country for the trip to not be too difficult for Ann to go. When we announced that she was going, the ladies in the church presented me with a check to cover her expenses. We flew into Mangalore, Kerala and spent our first night in a farmhouse. During the night, I felt something tickling my leg. I thought it was Ann. "Ann, I am too tired for love-making." She replied, "I haven't touched you." I jumped out of bed and slapped a house lizard off my leg. It was cool in the mountains and the lizard thought that my leg was a good place to get warm.

At the pastors' conference, Ann gave a lecture on the Christian family. Since it was not the custom for women to teach men in church, we excused the pastors and she talked to their wives. The pastors gathered around the windows, so they could hear what the American woman said. When she quoted scripture, saying, "Men, love your wives," the pastors roared with laughter. This was a new and ridiculous concept to them. In India, marriages are arranged by the parents, and telling your wife that you love her is perceived as unmanly. One pastor (upon recognizing that the New Testament teaches that husbands are to love their wives as Christ loved the church) went home, called his whole family together (including his two sons-in-law) and apologized to his wife for being an Indian husband and not a Christian one. Then, in front of the whole family, he embraced her and told her that he loved her. The Gospel is powerful. At the pastors' request, Ann's remarks at their conference were translated into Malayam for their future reference. On later trips, the pastors remained in the sessions when she taught.

One of the pastors in the room later started a church and named it the Ann Allen Chapel. The chapel in the children's home is also named for her. Her work contributed greatly to making the India Baptist Theological Seminary a place where the women study alongside the men and receive the same degree.

Soon, other churches joined in our efforts in India. Rev. Joe Burton, the pastor of the First Baptist Church of Radford, went with Tom Reynolds in 1983. Dr. Don Reid of Hillsville, Virginia went in 1986. Rev. Mark Jappe of California went in 1988 and spoke at the dedication of the building of Cherapurza Baptist Church. In 1989, Bill Ross went as part of his doctoral studies. At the time, he was the new pastor of the Vinton Baptist Church. Later, he and that church became a major partner in the India Mission.

In 1984, we also hosted a group that went to the Passion Play in Oberammergau, Germany. Even though the play was in German, we were able to follow and understand using an English translation. We had a full busload of travelers. Part of the group was led by Dr. Thomas Reynolds, my former associate in Blacksburg, who was then the pastor of the Harrisonburg Baptist Church. The trip ended in London. On the day of the city tour, I stayed home and did the laundry while Ann took the group on the tour. Normally, the hotel did the travel hosts' laundry as a courtesy. This hotel did not. I found a nearby laundrymat. When I went in, there were several elderly English ladies doing their laundry. They took the clothes from me. They remarked that a man did not know how to do laundry and proceeded to wash our clothes. I tried to pay for the machines. They refused, saying, "Your country saved us in World War II." They gave me the clothes neatly folded in a plastic bag. I took the bag and placed them neatly on the bed in the room. Folding clothes is not one of my skills. When Ann returned and saw that the clothes were folded up to her high standards, she asked, "What on earth happened?" There was no way I could have convinced her that I had folded the clothes, so I just told her the truth.

Dr. Reynolds took the group back to America. Ann, three other ladies, and I remained and took an eleven-day tour of England, Scotland, and Wales. Our trip through Europe had been a five-star trip. This tour was an economy trip. Naturally, I heard some grumbling, like, "I do not like to have to go out into the hall to turn my suitcase over." Since Ann and I both were experienced third-world travelers and the price was dirt cheap, we simply pointed out that a five-star trip would have been more than twice as expensive.

Ann and I got off the tour bus in the village of Thirsk and made our way to James Herriot's famous vet clinic. We arrived at 3:00 in the afternoon. A sign on the front door stated that Mr. Herriot received Americans at 2:00 p.m. Our hearts sank because we both had read and enjoyed all of his books. I said, "It does not say that that is the only time he sees Americans," and knocked on the door. He was at the clinic alone. He was a delightful and friendly man. He was gracious to us two rude Americans and gave us a private tour. He spent over an hour telling us stories of his life and family.

In 1986, Ann and I led a group to China. When we landed in Beijing, our guide, Jinlin Zhao, met us and told us that he had applied to a school in Virginia, called Virginia Tech. One of our travelers was a professor in the department he had applied to. In China, we visited all of the places tourists go, plus seminaries and churches. Zhao had difficulty understanding why we were so interested in churches. However, whenever we would fly, he would make the sign of the cross. I asked him why. He responded, "It makes me nervous to fly. I make the sign of the cross just in case you guys are right." Zhao came to Tech, completed his Ph.D., and today is a professor in Florida. We still get together from time to time. He and his wife and daughter are U.S. citizens.

To my surprise, in 1986, Dr. E. Bruce Heilman asked me to serve on the University of Richmond board of trustees for a second time. I was humbled and honored by this. Within the board, I served on the academic and honorary degree committees. I hope I made a contribution to the university. I know I learned a great deal from serving with these leaders of our state. By observing the many skills of Bruce Heilman, I learned much about leading an institution and about fundraising. He and I share similar backgrounds—having served in the military and then going to college. Needless to say, being a university pastor and serving on the board of one of our state's private universities was a status symbol in a university church like Blacksburg Baptist. Both Dr. Heilman and Dr. Lavery were kind enough to invite me to sit with them in the president's box when the two schools played each other. (The reader would find Bruce's remarkable life story worth reading: *An Interruption That Lasted a Lifetime*, Authorhouse.)

Katie, our younger daughter, was the scholar in our family. When she graduated from high school, many colleges contacted her, including the University of Richmond, which offered her a scholarship. She chose to follow her mother and her siblings to Radford University, where she graduated in June, 1989, and in the fall, began her teaching career in Gloucester, Virginia. (Later, she also earned a Master's degree from Radford.) In December, our family had an addition. She married Larry Forbish. Larry grew up in Wisconsin and Florida and graduated from the University of Illinois. He was beginning a career in finance and we were thrilled to have him in the family.

Meanwhile, our ministry to Chinese students was continuing to grow. Several became Christians and I baptized them in a ceremony with only Chinese present. Some were fearful that there would be problems for them if they became a church member. I also performed several weddings for them. When the Tiananmen Square protest in 1989 happened, some of the Chinese students in our church requested the use of our retreat center to have a meeting of student leaders. I agreed that they could use the center during their Christmas. After this meeting, some requested asylum. All of them became more open about being Christians.

"On one occasion, a Chinese visiting professor of electrical engineering was converted in the Friday night Bible study and made her profession of faith on Sunday morning. On Monday, she showed up at the church office asking that she be allowed to perform some service for Jesus. The secretary explained that there was no need for her to work at the church. She could do something kind for someone she knew. She insisted that she needed to perform some lowly service and would not leave until the secretary let her clean all of the women's bathrooms. Her story illustrates that in ministering to other cultures, as people come to Christ, they teach us new things about the faith and service." (Ray Allen, *Arms Reaching Around the World*, p.69, Center for Baptist Heritage & Studies, 2012.)

In the spring of 1990, Ann's stepfather, Francis Hamilton, passed away in our home. He had been a successful small businessman. Ann was the recipient of his estate. This enabled us to take some trips that we could never imagine before. It also enabled us to think about early retirement and a more relaxed second career.

In September, 1989, I completed 15 years as the pastor of Blacksburg Baptist Church. The church commissioned Robert Tuckwiller to paint an original work as a gift to Ann and me. Robert is our favorite artist. He painted a scene from the New River which we call Smallmouth Heaven. The New River is one of the world's most beautiful rivers and a famous smallmouth bass fishery. The picture hangs in the study of our home.

As the decade came to an end, the church was continuing to grow. It was involved in several cutting-edge ministries, such as the Chinese Bible study, and was sponsoring a Korean church, which worshipped in our sanctuary. Both of these continue to this day. We were on the radio twice each Sunday with many listeners. We entered the 1990's with a spirit of optimism.

A NEW DECADE

We began the new decade by raising a quarter of a million dollars to improve our facilities. One family gave the funds to paint the sanctuary. This cost 7,500 dollars. I warned the contractor he needed to do it in one week because if any part of the old paint remained, the people would say the paint had not covered. He assured us that he could do that but failed to finish the section under the balcony. Sure enough, a small group of ladies complained on Monday that the paint was not covering. I met with them, listened to them, and then suggested that since it would cost another $7500 to do it again, we should let him finish. Then, I explained that he would paint a section of the church with a second coat. If anyone could identify the area where the second coat was, then *we* would have to paint another coat. Only I and his workmen knew which area had two coats. No one could identify where the second coats were. Sometimes, seeing is believing.

The staff began to see that there needed to be a way to find out what the thinking of the members was and how they viewed the future. Bill Mashburn, a member and engineering professor, shared with me a planning process that he was using to help companies plan. He modified the plan, so that it could be used by a large group of people. The plan was to train the deacons to lead a small group in brainstorming the one thing our church should do. The ideas were placed on a blackboard. There was no debate, and after everyone had his say, a secret, weighted vote was taken (meaning each person voted five times for the idea he or she liked best, four times for their second favorite idea, and so on). Then all the groups came together. All of the top five ideas from each group were placed on newsprint around the room. The entire group (which was well over two hundred people) did the same weighted vote a final time. After the meeting, the group leaders turned in every idea that had been suggested by any member. The staff reviewed all of the results and concluded that there were excellent ideas that did not make the final five. A booklet was prepared listing all of the ideas and mailed to every member of the congregation.

The result was that the first thing on the mind of the congregation was to pay off the church debt. Since we had a low-interest loan and no difficulty in making the monthly payment, no one on the staff would have considered a campaign to pay off the debt. Immediately, we began planning the campaign to retire the debt. Grover Jones was vice-president of the bank we owed the money to, a former Tech football player, a choir member, and a very active member of our church. With his enthusiastic permission, the campaign became, *Let's Get Grover off of Ray's Back.* When the plan was presented at the business meeting, the congregation roared with laughter, voted to do it, and shortly thereafter, pledged to pay the debt within five years. They did it by the end of 1993.

March 2, 1991, was a big day for our family. Ray, Jr., married Melinda Fowler. Since he and Melinda were and are Republican consultants, there were many politicians and political consultants in attendance at the wedding. Sherman, our church maintenance supervisor, commented that with one hand grenade, he could have wiped out much of the Republican leadership in our state.

With things going well in the church, I decided that I would begin to take a month of my vacation during the summer. Until the 90's, I had taken only two weeks at a time, but as I grew older, I began to feel I needed a longer break to recharge my batteries. So in the summer of 1991, with Cecil and Carrie McBride, we set out on a five-week adventure: Hawaii, Australia, New Zealand, and Fiji. We planned to fly to the places on our schedule and have a hotel and car reserved. The travel agent that we booked through was the agency I had led many trips for, so they had my ticket flagged as a travel host. As a result, when available, we were bumped up to business or first class.

We arrived in Cains, Australia, at 6:00 in the morning. We picked up a car, and I had my first experience driving on the left side of the road. The difficulty was that the windshield wiper lever was located where the turn signal lever was on my car at home. Thus, when the windshield wipers came on, I knew I had not turned on the signal lights. Cecil commented, "I hope the natives know when they see an American going down the road with the windshield wipers on, he is going to make a turn."

I suspect most Americans assume Australians are just like us. They are wonderful people and very welcoming to Americans, yet they are very different from us. They are so laid back, we could learn from them. At first, as one who lived most days with appointments every thirty minutes, I was a little aggravated by this. Cecil and I made a reservation to go fishing. When we arrived, the guide did not have his boat in the water, nor had he caught the bait. We got the boat launched, caught the bait, and began fishing at 10:00 a.m. We assumed a half-day trip would end at noon, and we were wondering what we would do with the afternoon. We returned to the dock at 3:30 after a grand time of fellowship and fishing. The next day we were to go on a boat trip to the Great Barrier Reef. The tickets for the four of us, which cost $400, were supposed to be delivered to our hotel. They never arrived. The clerk said, "Just tell the boat captain what happened." We did, and he said, "No worries, welcome aboard." At Ayers Rock, we reserved a 15-minute helicopter ride over the rock. The pilot forgot the reservation, showed up an hour late, and gave us an hour's helicopter tour of the area. After I adjusted my attitude to theirs, it became a most unforgettable trip and I would love to go again.

We returned and entered a very busy fall. I had picked up ten pounds on our trip. Immediately, I reduced my calorie intake. Through the years, I had held my weight around what it had been when I was discharged from the army. Instead of losing, I gained five more pounds. I chalked it up to being older and redoubled my efforts to lose weight. Soon, I was sleeping more than normal and tired a great deal of the time. In late November, I went to the doctor. The normal blood tests did not show any problems. Since nothing appeared to be wrong, I did not go back to the doctor until mid-December. I self-diagnosed that I must be depressed. Dr. Robert Stockburger, who not only had been my physician for years, but is also a close friend and had roomed with me on many trips to India, knew me very well. I went to him and told him that since the blood tests indicated nothing was wrong, I probably needed an antidepressant. He disagreed and said he did not believe I was depressed. He checked me over and when he felt my throat, said, "That does not feel right; we need an MRI." Within a few days, I went for the MRI. All of my life, I have been able to force myself to do unpleasant things, but I could not stay in the MRI machine. So they scheduled a CT scan for the next morning. When the receptionist checked me in, she asked, "Dr. Allen, what are you doing back here?" I replied, "I flunked the closet phobia test." A solid mass was found in my thyroid. After consulting with several physicians, the decision was made to remove it quickly, which was done three days after it had been discovered.

The physicians warned me that often, adjusting to the Synthroid medication would take several months and that I should take it easy while that was being done. Like many men at 53 years old, I had rarely been sick, did not heed their advice, and in two weeks, was back in full swing. I had agreed to be the keynote speaker at the 200th anniversary celebration (in March of 1992) of William Carey's arriving in India as a Baptist missionary. I also agreed to write an article on William Carey for a publication of the Virginia Baptist Historical Society. I set to work preparing the article and the speech. I completed the article. But my own hardheadedness lengthened my recovery to the point that I did not feel up to the trip to India in March.

Gary Metcalf resigned to go to a church in Richmond. Joe Borden and I searched for his replacement and selected Deborah Christian. Debbie and her husband were both graduates of Virginia Tech. Debbie also had a master's degree from seminary.

Shortly after she joined, the entire staff, including the secretaries went to a conference in Philadelphia on taking a church past 800 in worship. We were at that point. The focus of the conference was that a church had to reorganize that it had to grow past that attendance level. We found many of the concepts helpful after baptizing some of them to fit BBC, and putting them to use.

We explored the idea that instead of having two identical worship services, we have three, each with a different style of worship. In laying our plans, we wanted to not disturb the folks who were coming and liked the church as it was. Since Sunday school had been the traditional place people experienced Bible study and fellowship, we planned a second Sunday school at the 11 o'clock hour. We sent lay people to study a church that had two successful Sunday schools. We were convinced that this was the wise way to deal with the limited space we had for Sunday school. Our proposal was that we change our schedule so that there was a worship service and a Sunday school at both 9:30 and 11:00 a.m.

Then the murmuring began. This would split families and keep them from worshipping together. It would be impossible to staff the Sunday school with good teachers. Where would people park? Some of my friends came and told me that things were going great, so do not change something that is working. "If it ain't broke, don't fix it." "Take more time off; you don't need to be working more, but less." Fortunately, the staff did not become an issue; it is hard to be critical of a staff that wants the organization to grow and wants to work more. The proposal was voted down overwhelmingly in the business meeting.

I learned it is almost impossible to get religious people to change their habits about coming to church. The way things have always been is the holy and only way for them to be. So if we came up with a way to continue to grow significantly, we had to leave Sunday as it was. At that point, on every Sunday, we had twice as many in worship as in Sunday school.

In January, 1992, I brought a proposal from the staff that we have a pilot project in worship, beginning on Palm Sunday, April 12th, and continuing through June 12th. The recommendation was that the 8:30 worship would be a traditional Baptist service with a tendency toward gospel music. The choir would sing the hymns most of us grew up with. An informal contemporary worship service would be added at 9:30 in an effort to reach people who had been turned off by traditional church, and further, that the 11:00 service would continue as a more formal worship. We requested that everyone continue to worship at the time they were worshipping and that the 9:30 be our outreach service. This passed with questions, but no objections.

The next crisis for that year came when a lady minister asked to be ordained. Traditionally, although not required, the ordaining church requests the local Baptist association to form an ordination council of the associational clergy. They question the candidate at length about their Christian experience and theology. She passed without any difficulty, which was something of a surprise because I knew that some of them did not agree with me on the ordination of women. A long-term deacon at BBC left the church in opposition to our ordaining her.

Our church was criticized when we began ordaining women deacons, and we expected more criticism for this than we received. My deeply held convictions were and are: that in the beginning, God created men and women. Throughout the universe, he created a male/female partnership. When one dominates the other, it is against the divine order and causes many problems. Men and women are different, and that is one of God's wonderful gifts. Paul writes, "In Christ, there is neither male nor female." (Gal. 3:28). Further, the first person called a deacon in the New Testament was a woman named Phoebe (Rom. 16:1). I concur with Randall Lolley when he says that the women were the last at the cross and the first at the tomb.

With many things happening in the church, we began the third worship service, a contemporary worship at 9:45, with around 100 in attendance. Members came to the new service. Some liked it; some made comments. My favorite comment was, "Our pep rally for Jesus service." I think he was saying that the service was too lively for his taste. Some said that if we continued the service, we would have Pentecostals coming to our church. The good thing was that people became Christians through the service and united with our church. In the fall, the church voted to continue with the three worship services and hired Kathy Breske, a local professional singer, to lead the music at 9:30. BBC continues to have three morning worship services today.

We concluded the year with over 100 voices singing in our Christmas musical, which was performed four times to accommodate all the people who wanted to attend. Dr. Joe Borden had developed the music ministry so that our Christmas musical became a community-wide event. The fellowship hall was packed for our annual Christmas party, and the Christmas Eve service was a full house.

In the summer, Ann and I decided to take a month's vacation and visit Alaska. We flew to Anchorage and rented a motor home. The goal was to see this great state, meet the people, and catch all five species of salmon. We fell in love with Alaska, I caught my goal of fish, and we rediscovered the fun of camping.

In the fall of 1992, I had been asked to serve as chairman of the Virginia Baptist General Board's Partnership Missions

Committee. In February, 1993, Tom Prevost, (our staff member for the committee) Stuart Carlton and I flew to Europe to seek places for our volunteers to work. Our first stop was Hungary. In 1947, the Baptist Women of Virginia had given Hungarian Baptists the money to build a girls' school in Budapest. When the communists took over, they confiscated the school and let North Korea use it as their embassy. When communism fell, the government gave the building back to the Hungarian Baptists. Since it was in need of repair, we decided to send volunteers to make the repairs.

Our next stop was Croatia. This new country had been devastated by war. We stayed in hotels where the upper floors had been blown away. Some of the world's most fertile land is in this beautiful country. We decided to send seeds, so the people could plant gardens. Our churches sent 67,000 video boxes full of garden and flower seeds. The flowers represented the beauty of Christian love. We named this ministry, *Seeds of Hope,* and it continued for a number of years. The committee received a letter from a Canadian volunteer on the ground stating that the flowers had made the countryside blue and that the Croatian people referred to the seeds as the "Baptist Seeds."

Our third stop was Sofia, Bulgaria. Perhaps no country suffered more than the Bulgarians under the communists. There, it was an honor for me to speak at the morning worship service of the Sofia Baptist Church, where Dr. Theo Angelov is pastor. Present at the service was the police officer who had arrested a previous pastor for preaching the Gospel.

Returning home, I found that the optimism of the congregation was extremely high. The staff decided to have another church-wide planning session. When all of the results were compiled, the number one suggestion was an expansion of our children's ministry, including the addition of a full-time professional children's minister to the staff.

The professional staff and I were in favor of hiring a children's minister, but we faced several difficulties. First, the seminaries were not currently training people in that specialty. Secondly, when we looked at the money, there was not enough to pay what a qualified person would expect. If a church is expanding rapidly, it is rarely more than a month away from bankruptcy.

A plan started to take shape. We had a large number of seniors and retirees moving to town who were regularly joining our church. They (as is the case with most churches) were our best source of funds. Yet most of them probably would not see the need for a children's minster. In order to make this work, we really needed to add two people, a children's minister and a seniors' minister. Since we could not afford either, it was a great plan.

So we began to write two job descriptions, beginning with the seniors' minister's position. This person would plan activities, ministries, and programs for people over 55. He or she would regularly visit this age group and share in the hospital visitations with the other ministers. He would advise the other ministers if there were members that they needed to call on.

The children's minister would plan activities, ministries, and programs for children and their families. This person would also share in the hospital visitations with the other ministers. (We already had the deacons visiting those in the hospital and the ministers visiting on a rotating basis, with one minister on call for holidays and weekends.) When the staff presented the plan to the church, it stipulated that for the first year only, the children's minister would be funded from the budget. The plan was approved.

After discussing it with Ann, she agreed that we could use some of the money she inherited from her stepfather to fund one-third of the salary for the seniors' minister. I had lunch with two of our successful businessmen, and they each agreed to give one-third also. The financial problem was solved.

After considering many applications, we settled on a person who had not applied. Jackie Byrd was a graduate of Radford University, a long-term member of the church, and one of the best elementary teachers in the school system. She had taught hundreds of children and was loved by them and their parents. She began her work with us in the summer and started a children's church called *Manna Street* in which she used the latest teaching methods. Soon, the children began to share with their classmates at school how much fun they were having in church, and kids poured in. She also planned activities for the families.

Shortly after Jackie came to work with us, a woman called from the jail and asked if a minister from our church could visit her. This was not uncommon because people in jail often listened to us on the radio. When Jackie introduced herself, the deputy on duty would not let her visit the inmate because he did not believe the Baptist church would have a female minister. The jailer's wife taught with my wife, Ann, and his wife knew Jackie. Before Jackie got back to the church, the jailer telephoned me, apologized for the deputy, and assured me that Jackie would be welcome to visit the jail any time she wanted to. Jackie was an excellent choice.

Dr. Don McKinney, who had been a year behind me in the doctoral program and had an extra year of clinical training, joined the staff in the fall. He loved seniors and was very faithful about visiting them in their homes. Don planned serious programs as well as fun trips for them. He was very loyal to me, and I always paid a visit to any senior he suggested needed a visit from the senior pastor. More seniors joined the church, and often, when Don would visit in their homes, the senior would give him an extra check to put in the offering. The plan was working.

Bringing two more professionals on board improved the ministry to our members and increased our outreach to the community. With our church having the only full-time children's minister and the only mainline church with a contemporary worship service, many new adults joined our fellowship. We were also using media advertising to attract people. Advertisements in the grocery section of the newspaper led to the town's leading grocery store owner and his family coming to our church. One of our best radio ads was of a child being interviewed and the announcer asking, *Do you go to the Blacksburg Baptist Church because you like the preaching? Child says: No! Do you go because you like the music? Child: No! Then why do you go? Child: Because I like the children's story! Come worship with us on Sunday; you will like the children's story, too.*

Early in 1994, it became obvious that we needed more space, so a planning committee was appointed to create more Sunday school space and add a family life center. I knew this was needed, but frankly, I did not look forward to going through the process of raising money and the long hours a pastor spends when he is leading a congregation through a large building program. I had been through four building programs at Blacksburg.

Ann and I went on a month's RV trip out west in midsummer of 1994. We talked about a lot of things. Our lives had been extremely busy. Ann was teaching. I was serving a large university church, was one of the leaders in our Virginia Baptist missions program, and was leading the ministry in India. My plate was very full. We talked about wanting more time to enjoy life. We questioned whether the church would be better-led if a young person with more energy were pastor. On the trip, we decided to retire in January, 1995, and after a long break, pursue other ministries.

At the business meeting in October, we announced our decision to the church. The officers of the deacons' committee came the next day and convinced me to wait until at least June to retire. They returned in January of 1995 and asked me not to retire; I thanked them but stuck with our plan.

During the late winter and spring of 1995, I explored what I might do for a second career. I talked at length with a seminary about teaching. The executive director of Virginia Baptist talked with me about becoming a consultant for international missions. Both of these positions required me to start work in the fall of 1995. We were having supper with our son's family and discussing our possibilities with him. He said, "Dad, if you take any job right after you retire, you will be right back to working as hard as ever. Do nothing for at least a year." We took his advice and decided to sell our home in Blacksburg, put our stuff in storage, and travel in our RV for a year.

Meanwhile, in April of 1995, Virginia Baptist asked me to be a part of the team exploring what mission projects they might undertake in Panama. The day before we left, Dr. McDonough, the executive director, became ill and asked me to lead the team. We landed in Panama City on a Monday, late in the evening. The missionary shook hands with me and said, "Dr. Allen, I understand you like to fish." I nodded my head and he continued, "We have a guide reserved to take you fishing Thursday morning. You catch the Peacock bass, and we will have a fish fry for the mission station on the last night you are here." I thought he was kidding, but he was not.

At 4 o'clock Thursday morning, a missionary took me to the lake that is used to fill the locks for the Panama Canal. Our guide spoke only Spanish. His fishing rod and reel was a metal coke can with fishing line wrapped around it. The fishing was unbelievable. We caught over 90 bass. There are no limits in Panama, so we could keep all of them. After such good luck, I asked that they arrange a second trip for me. The catch was more than enough to feed the entire mission station. One of the projects we did grew out of our fishing experience. We learned that some of the native pastors were having to row from island to island to preach in dug-out canoes. When we returned, we purchased outboard motors for the pastors.

The last few months in Blacksburg flew by. The church planned and did many things to make the time a good one. They planned a great retirement party and took care to invite my friends, Dr. McDonough and Dr. Rhodenhiser to speak. They presented me with a fine computer and established an endowed mission named for Ann and me which funds international missions' projects.

Many pastors write an interesting article for every newsletter their church sends out. I only wrote an article when I wanted to call the congregation's attention to something or share some thoughts. I wish to end this section of my story with an article I wrote in the spring of 1992 and which Jim Massey included in his *History of Blacksburg Baptist Church, 1852-1992* on page 155:

"Somehow we must return to the simple.

We must muster the courage to know again that...living within our means is the only way to live long.

Further, if you travel light, you have less fatigue.

Happiness is two people in love snuggled together. It has nothing to do with the cost of the bed.

Joy is a child asleep in granddaddy's arms.

The first job as parents is to raise the child.

If they fail at that, they are a failure.

The best schools have a caring teacher, an eager pupil, a slate and a piece of chalk.

To date, all of our heroes have graduated from that kind of school.

Good government keeps the streets safe and fixes the potholes.

The most efficient health plan is to have a clear mind, a lean body, monogamous sex, no alcohol and no drugs.

The prudent know if you do not observe the Sabbath, the Creator will put you on a permanent rest.

Wisdom is knowing, in the end, we all get the same amount of real estate.

REFLECTIONS ON BLACKSBURG

This is difficult to write. How do you reflect with reasonable brevity on over 20 years of your life?

Blacksburg Baptist and the town of Blacksburg were wonderful places to raise a family. The church allowed Ann and me and our children to be ourselves, without ever pressing us to be different because I was the pastor.

They gave me complete freedom to preach as I saw fit and were always encouraging me as a speaker. When I became involved in denominational activities or international ministries, they encouraged me and made sure my expenses were paid. They respected our family having time as a family. Not once in the 21 years there did they have me come home from vacation to respond to an emergency. They would advise me of the emergency and assure me that one of the associate pastors was handling it well, and that I need not be concerned.

They allowed me two sabbatical leaves to teach at Southeastern Seminary. They also allowed time for two of our associate pastors to complete their doctoral studies while working on our staff.

During my retirement, they have funded many of the mission projects that I have been involved in. Tom McDearis, my successor, has become a dear friend. In 2002, they made me Pastor Emeritus. Whenever they have invited me to fill the pulpit, they have treated us as if we had never left.

Thanks for blessing our lives with your love.

RETIREMENT AND A SECOND CAREER

On June 9, 1995, we set out for Alaska. When we started down the west side of Bushy Mountain, we both had a deep sadness, for we were leaving behind the major portion of our life, yet there was a keen sense of adventure as we began a new stage. Probably our children thought that their parents were having a second childhood in midlife.

We were traveling in a 1994 white, Dodge pickup with a fold-up portable boat on top and pulling a Sunnybrook travel trailer. Our trip plan was to drive through Michigan, across Wisconsin, through Minnesota and North Dakota, across Canada, and on to Alaska; then to return through the Northwest to complete visiting all of the 50 states. Since we planned to RV for a year, we were not in a hurry.

In about fifteen days, we reached Dawson Creek and began to drive the Alaska Highway. This highway is one of the most remarkable engineering achievements of World War II. After the attack on Pearl Harbor, the road was built to provide a link between the lower 48 and Alaska. Construction began on March 8, 1942, and it was completed eight months and twelve days later on October 25, 1942. Today, the road is paved all the way to Fairbanks. This is one of the great drives in the entire world. Wildlife abounds. When we had seen thirty bears, we quit counting.

There are too many interesting things to mention about traveling along the road. We took them all in. Our first major stop was at Watson Lake. In 1942, a soldier, Carl Lindley of Danville, Illinois, hung a sign on a post with the name of his hometown on it, beginning the famous Sign Post Forest. Over 30,000 people have posted their signs. Since our house had closed the day we arrived and our only home was our trailer, our sign read, "The Allens from VA."

We reached Skagway, Alaska on Sunday, July 2nd. We had planned to go to the Baptist church. We were unaware that Alaska was on daylight savings time and Canada was on standard time. At 10:50 a.m., we found ourselves in front of the Presbyterian church. We parked our rig, which was over 50 feet long, and went to church. This turned out to be a wonderful church experience. The church was in the middle of a building program. The place was packed. When the offering time came, the pastor told us he did not want us to contribute. We were guests of the church and the members took care of the expenses of the church.

Skagway was of particular interest to me because a distant cousin of mine went there during the Klondike gold rush seeking his fortune. He apparently found some gold, because he returned to southwest Virginia and built an expensive house. We took in all of the attractions of the gold rush and spent considerable time in the cemetery, where we found some Allen tombstones.

Our next major stop was the fascinating town of Tok. The town in 1995 had a little over 1,200 people but no government, no police department, and no taxes. When things needed to be done, the citizens got together and did them. We cleaned our rig and greatly enjoyed the singing groups that performed in the RV park.

We continued up the Alaska Highway to Fairbanks, the second largest city in Alaska. The University of Alaska has a wonderful museum of Arctic artifacts there. Their animal research station is also nearby, where we observed the animals of Alaska. Fairbanks is the place where most of the materials bound for the oilfields depart from on trucks that travel the Dalton Highway. Nearby is the second largest gold mine in the world.

Leaving Fairbanks, we headed south to Denali. After an early morning bus tour through Denali National Park and a stop in Anchorage, we made our way to Hope to fish for a week or so. To our surprise, the owner of the campground and the postmistress remembered us from our previous trip. In church, the pastor welcomed us back. This is one of our favorite places. Main Street is a dirt road. Some of the people still earn their living panning gold from Resurrection Creek. A moose or a bear is often seen within town limits. All varieties of salmon swim into the creek to spawn.

We had two experiences there that still stick in my memory. The first experience was that each morning when I went fishing, I would notice an elderly gentleman who fished nearby. Two mornings a week, he and his wife would leave in their car and not return until evening. As we visited on the creek bank, I inquired as to how his wife was doing. He said, "Not well." Then he shared with me that she had cancer and was going to Anchorage for treatment. They had loved to travel in their RV and when it became obvious she was not going to beat the cancer, they decided to take one last trip to Alaska. The plan was that when she died, he would have her cremated, fly home with her ashes, have the funeral with the children, return and complete the trip. What a great way to deal with the loss of a long-term love.

The second experience involved the five-year-old son of a soldier who was stationed in Alaska. The family arrived in a rented pop-up camper for the weekend. They had stopped in Anchorage and bought inexpensive rods and reels. I saw them arrive and get set up. The soldier and his son came to the creek to fish while the wife fixed supper. The father went about 200 feet past me, but the boy stopped to see a nice salmon I had caught for our supper. Soon, he soon was casting as close to me as he could get. I got a nice fish on and asked him if he wanted to land the fish, which he did with a great deal of skill for a five-year-old. He asked, "Mr., what are you going to do with your fish?" I replied, "You landed it. It's your fish." It was difficult to learn to hook salmon on my first trip to Alaska. I spent a very frustrating day learning how. This boy caught on immediately and soon had a limit of five fish on the bank. His mother called him and his father for supper. As his father walked up the bank empty-handed, the boy shouted, "Daddy, come help me carry my fish." The next morning when I stepped out of my camper, my new best friend was waiting, and with a million-dollar smile, asked, "Mr. Allen, what time are we going fishing?"

After a couple of weeks in Hope, we went on to Kenai Lake Federal RV Park. As we were setting up, the campground host chased a black bear out of the park with a broom. A native Alaskan was camping beside us. He invited me to fish with him in a creek nearby that had a lot of trout in it. Ann told me to bring back two for supper. Soon, I had two trout cleaned and hanging on a tree branch for our supper. Since the fishing was excellent, I continued to fish, but released them. When I was ready to go, I turned and my fish were gone. There on the ground were the large tracks of a grizzly bear leading up to the tree where I had hung my fish. The bear had sneaked up to within ten feet of me and stolen my fish. I am glad I did not see him. That night, a grizzly and a moose got in a fight and turned over the tent two fishermen were sleeping in. Bears are an almost daily part of summer life in Alaska.

After over a month of bird-watching and fishing on the Kenai Peninsula, we returned to Anchorage to meet two of our friends, Cecil and Carrie McBride, who flew up to visit us for a couple of weeks. Since Cecil and Carrie had earlier visited friends in Alaska, they wanted to spend time with us and catch some fish. The couple beside us in the campground in Alaska was John and Jane Doe (not their real names).

Normally, I go to church every Sunday but when we arrived at Ninilchik, the only time we could book a halibut trip was on a Sunday. So I missed church and went fishing. God has such a sense of humor—the sea was rough and I spent the day seasick chumming over the side of the ship.

Next, we went to Seward to fish for silver salmon. John and Jane arrived unplanned at the same campground that we were in.

On the way back to Anchorage to take the McBrides to the airport, we stopped at Potter Marsh to bird watch, but the birds had already flown south. When we reached the RV Park, the Does were already there.

It was Labor Day. The campground had several hundred sites, but by evening, there were few campers left. The campers and the birds had all headed south for the winter. In the morning, we shared our plans with the Does to go to the Alaska state fair and then head south. We agreed that we would meet at Johnson's Junction and drive the Cassiar Highway together.

The highway, which at the time was mostly a gravel road, proved to be a great adventure. Along the way, there were too many lakes and streams to fish all of them, but John and I often put the boat in and caught trout and salmon. RVers' unwritten code is not to ask another one what their vocation is or was. Nor did I volunteer that I was a retired pastor because the image of a pastor is that he is a killjoy. I found that if they got to know me as a person, then learned that I was a minister, we could have a normal man-to-man relationship. John had been many places outside the U.S., and we often spoke of being in such and such country, but did not mention why we were there. One day, while John and I were off fishing, Jane asked Ann what I did to earn our living. Ann told her and her response was, "John said, 'He was some kind of missionary or something.'" Then she shared that John had been an FBI agent for over 35 years. Laughing at supper, he said, "Ray, if you think telling people you were a Baptist preacher makes them not want to fish with you, try telling them you are a former FBI agent. They think you will put them in jail, and I have not arrested anyone in five years." They both sang in the choir in their church back home.

One great stop was Houston, British Columbia. The town claims to be the Trout Fishing Capital of the World. We pulled into the Shady Grove Campground for the night. A man in beat-up jeans was operating a backhoe. He stopped, got off, and assisted us with parking our rigs. We thought he was the handyman, the owner. He volunteered to take us fishing after supper and showed up with a beat-up old Sears Vee Boat in the back of a 20-year-old pickup. He drove to the airport, drove across the runway, unlocked a gate, and drove us to the lake where they landed float planes. His outboard was a sputtering, ancient, loud, Sears air-cooled motor. We trolled and soon had ten beautiful trout, each four to eight pounds.

He and his wife were very interesting and successful people. In addition to owning a lot of real estate, also had a business building roads for the logging industry. On a later trip returning from Alaska, we spent a week with them, and he took us deep into the wilderness, where we fished lakes that possibly had never been fished before. On one lake, I caught 16 cutthroat trout on 16 consecutive casts. Near that lake, over 20 miles from a normal road, I also saw a mother lynx and her two cubs.

In mid-September, we arrived in Banff, Canada. Our plan was only to stay there a couple of days and come back into the U.S. in Idaho. The Does stayed one more night and headed back home. We enjoyed this high Rockies town very much. Elk walk downtown and the campground was full of these magnificent animals. On the evening of our second day in town, we squared things away, planning to depart in the morning. Morning arrived with three inches of snow, so our departure was delayed a couple more days.

We crossed the border into Idaho and headed west toward Seattle, Washington. As we approached the city, I looked up and saw a 747 about 100 feet about the truck coming in for a landing. We were beside the Boeing airfield where they checked pilots out on the new planes. We parked and watched the jumbo jets flying around, landing and taking off like Piper Cubs at an air show.

In the Seattle area, we particularly wanted to see the damage done by the eruption of Mt. St. Helens, visit Mt. Hood in Oregon, and take some pictures of Mt. Rainier. On our second day there, I went to the barbershop. One of the customers, recognizing my southern accent inquired as to what I was doing in Seattle. I told him and he said, "My advice to you is hook up and leave, because it's going to start raining tomorrow and it will not quit until next summer." His prediction was correct, as the next morning, it began to rain and a heavy fog rolled in. We waited a week for it to clear and it did not. We only saw the top of Mt. Rainier when we flew home for me to attend a board meeting.

We were in Virginia for two weeks attending the board meeting and visiting friends. Our plane tickets were purchased using frequent flier miles, and we experienced poor service and rudeness from airline employees for the first time. One told me that if he had his way, there would be no such thing as frequent flier tickets. I reminded him that I had flown over 100,000 miles to earn those tickets and that perhaps he would not have a job if people like me did not fly with his airline. After having flown countless miles, I now avoid flying, if possible. It's amazing how the airline personnel and others do not make the connection, "customer equals jobs."

Back in Seattle, we continued down the west coast and started back across country through Arizona, New Mexico, and Texas. Our plan was to spend a week or so trout fishing in Cotter, Arkansas, but a record cold front hit the southern states. We decided to go home, park our rig, and take in the Christmas shows in Branson, Missouri instead.

REFLECTING ON THIS TRIP

Being a full time RVer is an excellent way to begin the transition from a busy career to a more relaxed retirement and second career. By talking with people in America and Canada, we returned from this trip greatly encouraged. We met some wonderful people in both countries. The churches and the people were amazing. We visited many different denominations. People wanted to take us home for lunch. We always thanked them and declined. They would then direct us to the best restaurants in town.

FLORIDA, HERE WE COME

On Christmas Day, 1995, Ann and I headed to Florida. It was about 10 degrees when we left Smith Mountain Lake. It did not get above freezing until we crossed into Georgia on the 26th. Our two daughters and their families followed us the day after Christmas. Our first stop was Cedar Key, Florida, where we rented a condominium for them to stay in and spent a chilly week swimming with the manatees. On New Year's Day, they returned to Virginia and we headed to Clewiston, Florida.

While home during Christmas, we bought a used van and Ann pulled our 20 foot deck boat to Florida. We stayed the first two weeks in Roland Martin's Campground. It was fairly new and had almost no trees. When you have a nice boat, a lot of people in an RV park want to fish with you. Soon, I was catching a lot of nice bass. We decided that we wanted to finish the winter in Clewiston. So we began to look for a campground with larger sites and trees.

We found the Crooked Hook RV Resort, which is a beautiful place about three miles south of town. The people there welcomed us with open arms. As previously mentioned, we never shared with people that I was a Baptist minister. We attended the campground service, which was led by the Rev. Rod Ruby, a Methodist minister. He and his wife, Lida, became our dear friends.

Within a month, he invited me to speak at the services. To everyone at the park, we were Ray and Ann, and are to this day. Sometimes, they affectionately call me the Bassin' Man, and Ann, the Bird Lady. We earned both of these titles. I earned mine by winning the park bass tournament several times. It was a little upsetting to those men who somehow feel that Baptist preachers are not quite he-men. I won it the first two times I fished in it. But the third time was even worse for them when Ann won the tournament. Ann is a walking encyclopedia on birds, hence her appropriate nickname.

After spending a great three months in Florida, we returned to our campsite at Smith Mountain Lake. In the month of May, I did repairs on our rental property and caught up with family and friends.

In June, we headed north to spend the summer in the Thousand Islands area between New York and Canada. We still had not answered the question, "What were we going to do with the remainder of our lives?" Some were probably asking, "What is Ray going to do if he ever grows up?" Relatives were asking, "You're really not going to do this RV thing the rest of your life, are you?" While older relatives thought that maybe we had lost it, our grandchildren thought it was rather neat. Our grandchildren Michael and Rebecca went to Thousand Islands with us for a couple of weeks.

The only noteworthy thing about the trip was that Michael and I almost got arrested. It is very windy on the water in the Thousand Islands area. One day, Michael and I decided to get a kite and fly it from the boat. We tied the kite to my largest fishing reel which had over 200 yards of line on it. In the wind, the kite soared to the full extent of the line, over 600 feet. The Canadians on shore were waving and motioning for us to come back. We thought they were cheering us on, so we returned to the dock to figure out a way to go even higher. They were waving to warn us that it's against the law in that area to fly a kite over 200 feet in the air. Fortunately, no one called the police.

In September, Dr. Reggie McDonough, the executive director of Virginia Baptist, telephoned me. He said the Lynn Haven Baptist Church in Vinton, Virginia had been through a difficult time and needed a strong leader to be the interim pastor. Further, he wanted to recommend me for the position. After a lengthy discussion, I agreed that he could give them my name, but that we would not be available until November 1st.

We had a lot of thinking and talking to do before we went back to work. First, did I want to work full or part time? Second, did we want to do this interim and then return to being full-time RVers? Did we want to live in our RV or buy a house? We both loved being the pastor of a church, but the 14 months we had traveled were certainly one of the better times of our life. We had missed seeing the children and grandchildren and also being in a local church. We both missed some of the things you have in a house but do not have in an RV. I missed having a woodworking shop. By the time we returned to Virginia, the decisions had been made. We would have a second career doing interim work. We would keep our RV and go to Florida between interims, and buy a house with some land.

A SECOND CAREER

Baptist churches call and employ their own pastors. This means there are several months and sometimes as much as a couple of years before they choose a new pastor. Usually, they call an interim pastor, who is often a retired pastor. He performs the normal duties of a pastor while the church deals with any major problems in the life of the congregation. He also assists the pastoral search committee in finding a new pastor. Today, there is special training available and some are making this work their careers.

Our interim at the Lynn Haven Baptist Church began on the first of November, 1996. I agreed that I would work four days per week and be available for weddings and funerals. The church had some difficulty with their relationship with the last pastor and he had started a new church. A significant number of members had left Lynn Haven. Some of the leadership felt that the focus of the interim should be on getting back those who had left. I resisted this, saying that the best course was to let them be. I said, "If they choose to return, welcome them back, but do not make a big deal of this." Some did return, but most did not.

Shortly after we began the interim, we purchased a house that was under construction in rural Bedford County. The house was built on a lot containing almost three acres of wooded land. We moved in on December 20, 1996.

Using the planning process I had developed in Blacksburg, the church redefined its mission and set some realistic goals. Some of the enthusiasm returned to the congregation, and attendance and financial support increased. Ann sang in the choir, and we found ourselves enjoying the same position we had enjoyed most of our adult life.

As is often the case during an interim, other staff members resign and take positions elsewhere. The minister of music, who was also the seniors' minister, resigned. I suggested to the leadership that we separate the two positions and hire a part-time person as interim and let the new pastor decide how he wanted to configure the staff. They agreed, and I invited Dr. Robert Wayne, one of the church's former pastors, to be the seniors' minister, and Joy Wright to be the choir director. Both of them are very talented people and did outstanding jobs.

While at Lynn Haven, two special family events occurred. On July 18, 1997, we welcomed our third granddaughter into the family. Jennifer Marie Allen is the older child of our son, Ray, Jr., and his wife, Melinda. We also gave Ann a surprise party for her 60th birthday. The governor declared it Ann Allen Day in Virginia and sent her a certificate of recognition citing her service as a teacher, mother, and missionary. It was a great thrill, much like the time when the Precious Children's Home in India named their chapel in her honor.

We were at Lynn Haven for 14 months when the new pastor arrived. This was a good experience, and we made many new friends. One thing that happened that I had never experienced was that seven people in the congregation died. Every one of them died on a Thursday. This meant that their funerals were on a Saturday. I share this because when I was discharged from the army, I said that I was not going to work on Saturdays. The truth is that on most Saturdays, a pastor finds himself doing a wedding or a funeral.

We packed up and headed to Florida for the spring. A few days after we set up at Crooked Hook, I received a telephone, from Dr. Earle Moore, a successful physician in Chase City, Virginia. He identified himself as a lowly freshman at the University of Richmond when I was a senior. He shared that his church had had some trouble, and they wanted me to come and be the interim pastor. I told him we were in Florida, and that I had agreed to speak at the community Easter sunrise service. I suggested several other people who were available. Assuming that he would get one of them, I did not think any more about it.

The Monday after Easter, he called me again. I inquired if he had found an interim. He replied, "Yes, you. The committee decided to wait until you returned." I agreed to come spend a weekend and discuss the possibility with them. My concern was that the church was 100 miles away from where we lived and it would require our staying many nights away from home. And not since my pastorate at Wise Baptist had I served as the only staff member.

We found the people delightful. We accepted the position. We were to come to Chase City on a Saturday night, stay in the parsonage, work through Tuesday, and be home Wednesday through Saturday. On our first Saturday, there was a note on the door of the parsonage. Several of them were gathering at a member's house and having a picnic. They hoped we could come. Chase City was my most enjoyable interim. We have never been fed so much wonderful home cooking. Many of the members had farm ponds, and they invited me to fish in them.

The first deacons' meeting I attended as interim pastor was perhaps one of the most interesting I have ever attended. The chairman asked each deacon to share something he was thankful for as the devotional to begin the meeting. Johnny, a WWII veteran, without cracking a smile, said, "A pint of bourbon." The chairman asked, "Would you mind explaining that?" Johnny shared that when he hit the beach on D-Day, he had hidden a pint of bourbon in his pack. Several days later, he was in a foxhole playing cards with his buddies. He remembered his bourbon and crawled back to his foxhole to have a drink. While there, a shell came in, hit the foxhole he had just left his buddies in, and they were all killed. "The bourbon saved my life, and I thank God every day of my life for it."

In September, we put the church through the BBC planning process. The church building had been built before WWII when most of the members were young. There was a men's room and ladies' room on the main floor. The only problem was that there was only one commode in each of the restrooms. Bathrooms are a big issue for seniors. Every woman in the church put down as one of their priorities to have a larger ladies' room on the main floor.

On Monday morning after reviewing all of the responses, I asked the chairman of the property committee to come to the office. We discussed the needs and walked through the building. When they had previously remodeled, they had left the old church kitchen as a storage space. We took measurements and discovered that it was large enough to build a ladies' room with four commodes and a nice lounge area. At the next business meeting, the church voted unanimously to proceed with the construction. At the meeting, the ladies made the point that I was the only one who had listened to their complaints, and some suggested the church name it the Ray Allen Ladies' Room. I told them that I was deeply moved, but with deep appreciation, wished to decline the honor.

In January, 1999, Ann and I made our first trip to India since retirement. On that trip, Dr. Earle Moore and his wife, Janice, accompanied us to hold medical clinics. A group consisting of eight students and the professor of missions, Dr. Isam Ballenger from the Baptist Theological Seminary in Richmond, completed the team. The students went to paint a building at the India Baptist Theological Seminary. Each student had the opportunity to preach in an evangelistic crusade.

On our first workday in India, I went with Dr. Moore to purchase medicine. Later, when he returned to the medicine shop, the owner asked why his father had not returned to help him with the selection of the medicine. He delighted in telling me this since he is only four years younger than I.

The doctors were outstanding in the clinics. Dr. Moore holding a clinic in their first aid station on a tea plantation, which was supervised by an Indian doctor. The manager of the plantation had not told his doctor that we were coming. He was justly upset. By the time we arrived, approximately two hundred patients had lined up to see the American doctor. I met with the Indian doctor and suggested that he sit with our Dr. Moore and assist him with the patients. Whenever he diagnosed a problem and prescribed a medication, he first conferred with the Indian doctor. At the end of the clinic, the Indian doctor asked our Dr. Moore if he would examine each of his family members.

The four of us traveled by train to Bangalore. There, we were joined by Dr. Stockburger and my successor at Blacksburg Baptist, Dr. Tommy McDearis. The physicians held clinics while Dr. McDearis and I spoke at a pastors' conference. This was Tommy's first trip to India. Indians, when they are listening and agreeing with you, shake their heads from side to side similar to how an American shakes his head to disagree. We forgot to tell him this. When he finished, he asked me, "How on earth could they disagree with everything I said?" When I burst out in laughter, he said. "Ray, this is not funny." He was greatly relieved when I explained they were expressing agreement with everything he had said.

First Baptist Church of Chase City had always called a young man as pastor, which was a wise thing to do when they had many young people in the congregation. Today, however, most of their members were over 50. I suggested that they increase the salary (which they could easily afford) and call a man at the end of his career. They took the advice and called Gene Burris, a chaplain at Roanoke Memorial Hospital. He was in his late 50's and remained the pastor until he retired.

I had the good fortune to be asked by Duke Divinity School to serve on the board of the Baptist House of Studies. While in Chase City, I recruited Dr. Earle Moore and Patricia Garland, vice-president of Estes Trucking Company in Richmond, to serve on the board. Later "The Jimmy and Helen Garland Scholarship," which aids a worthy Baptist student to attend Duke Divinity School. My final two years on the board, I served as chairman and we added several more scholarships. When I completed my term, there were 100 Baptist seminary students at Duke.

The summer of 1999, we completed the interim at Chase City. We spent the summer finishing a woodworking shop and a room in the basement of our house. That fall, we returned to Florida for the winter. In February, 2000, we returned to do the interim at Grandin Court Baptist Church in Roanoke.

The church had been a very strong church, but over the previous decade had declined rapidly. The pastor had been asked to leave. The church had, in the past, attracted some of the business leaders of the city. It was in an excellent location and had beautiful, well-maintained facilities. Through the years, the church had saved up over a half million dollars and continued to attempt to save money. When asked about this, they always replied that this was their "rainy day" fund.

As they prepared their budget, I told the committee that they should establish how much money would be required in savings to save a church, and then add a thousand dollars to pay someone to straighten up and lock up the buildings after the church died. They continued to go around the room discussing the budget. Then the chairman stopped and asked me, "Ray, are you trying to tell us something?" I responded, "You cannot save a church with money. Why should members give to transfer money from their savings accounts to the church's savings account? The members give their money to be spent in reaching people and ministering to the community." His response was, "Blacksburg was a larger church than ours. How much money did you keep in reserves?" I responded softly, "Nothing—we lived Sunday to Sunday." He asked, "What did you do if the furnace broke down." My response, "It broke down many times. I wrote the people a letter saying, 'The furnace is broken, and if we are going to have it fixed, please give extra this Sunday.' They never failed to dig a little deeper and respond not only to repair the furnace, but also to any other need that we had. A church lives or dies on its faith in Christ and its trust in its members." He shocked me with his response, "What should we do?" My reply, "Three things—stop saving money; put $1,000 per month in the new budget for the new pastor to spend on outreach; and rather than putting a figure down for the new pastor's salary, tell the congregation it will be whatever it takes to employ a pastor who has the skills to lead the people forward." They voted unanimously to do what I suggested.

Then the pastor search committee approached me and asked me to recommend a person I felt could do the job. Without hesitation, I recommended Kevin Meadows, who had been the youth minister with Bill Ross at Vinton Baptist Church. At the time, he was doing an outstanding job in a growing church in North Carolina. I pointed out that Kevin was serving a larger church than Grandin Court and probably was making an excellent salary. Further, because of his success early in his career, much larger churches would no doubt be looking at him. If he agreed to be considered, their job would be to sell him on the opportunity.

They went to hear Kevin preach and talked at length with him. Naturally, he called me with a barrel of questions. One thing I remember that I told him was that the church had been in survival mode for several years, but I felt that they had made a giant step forward in considering him, and I believed he could do the job if he chose to accept. He accepted beginning in January, 2001. In many ways, this was my most successful interim. Under Kevin's leadership, Grandin Court experienced a dramatic turnaround. It has grown, continues to grow significantly each year, and has become involved in ministries around the world.

As soon as it was known that Kevin was coming to Grandin Court, Vinton Baptist Church approached me about doing their interim. Bill Ross, my former youth minister, had been their pastor for over ten years. We had joined the church after Blacksburg had called a new pastor, so it would be clear to all that we were not going to return and live there. Ann Cranwell, our oldest, and her family had been very active members there for a number of years. I talked with her before accepting the position. Her response was that I had been her pastor longer than anyone else. For me, this was the first time that I would be the pastor for Michael and Rebecca, her children and our grandchildren, both of whom were very active in the youth program.

The committee assured me that they were going to move rapidly on securing a new pastor, and the interim would likely only last six months. Nevertheless, I made it clear that I was starting their job without a break and would take a vacation in the summer. Since they had been actively involved in the India mission, they were comfortable with my going to India the last of January. We spent the first three weeks at the church, then went to India.

Ann, Jesse Taylor (the custodian at Grandin Court Baptist), and I were the entire mission team. Jesse, who had grown up in an orphanage and spent some time in prison as a youth, was a tremendous success with the children in the children's home and in the prisons. His testimony of how he became a new person in Christ is deeply moving.

Vinton Baptist was the first church I had served in my entire ministry where there had not been some difficulty between the pastor and the congregation that led to his leaving. Bill had been well-loved by the congregation and had seen the church grow under his ministry from a thousand members to two thousand members. I thought the committee was mistaken in thinking that they would have a new pastor in six months, but I also thought it would be an easy interim and likely not last more than a year.

On January 28, 2001, we welcomed our second grandson, Matthew Reid Allen. He is the son of Ray and Melinda. We now had someone to carry forth the Allen name.

The youth minister at Vinton Baptist resigned before I arrived, and shortly after I returned from India, the minister of education and seniors also resigned. I discussed at length with the leadership that we should fill these with interims and make it clear that they would not be considered for the permanent positions. The bookkeeper also resigned, but I saw no reason not to seek a permanent bookkeeper. We hired a college student, Eric Slusher, to be the youth minister, and I was able to persuade Dr. Robert Wayne to come as minister to seniors. They both did excellent jobs for us.

My grandchildren all call me Granddaddy Ray, and soon all of the youth in the church were calling me that as well. Later, my grandson's best friend, Adam Phlegar, entered the ministry. After seminary, he asked me to preach his ordination sermon and go with him to be questioned by the council. He kept referring to me as Granddaddy Ray, and after his questioning session, another minister stated that he did not know that I had such a fine grandson in the ministry. I assured him that I would be proud to have Adam as a grandson, but that he was my grandson's best friend.

As I drove to work on the morning of September 11, 2001, I heard the report of the planes crashing into the twin towers in New York. By the time I reached the church office, the staff had a television set up, so we could keep up with what was happening. My feelings were a combination of grief for the lives lost and anger at those who had committed this horrible crime. As is the case in all tragedies, the pastor must put his own feelings aside and comfort others. Since the members knew I had been in several Arabic countries, I probably got more questions from them about Islam than most pastors. The youth responded in a way that was surprising to me. They asked that I meet with them on the Sunday after 9/11. They assumed that there was going to be a big war, and that they would have to fight in it. From my grandchildren, they knew that I had been a soldier. They asked questions about being a soldier and what it was like to kill somebody, which I could not answer because I had never been in combat. I did my best to reassure them as I had reassured the church in the morning worship services.

A few Sundays after 9/11, we invited the policeman and fireman of the community to come and worship with us, so we could express our appreciation to them. Most of our town's first responders came and it was a great time for them as well as for the congregation.

As is often the case in times of national crisis, people come back to the church. During the interim, the attendance did not decline. The giving actually increased and the church did over $200,000 in organ improvements and began a remodeling of the sanctuary.

On July 4, 2002, the church had a record attendance. Some of the veterans gave their testimony. We recognized the veterans with a certificate of appreciation. The service ended with four active servicemen on the platform, and the vets saluting their fellow servicemen who were on active duty. There was not a dry eye in the house when it was over.

The interim that was supposed to last only six months lasted 25 months. The search committee looked at well over 100 ministers. Finally, they chose Dr. Bill Booth, who was serving a much smaller church in southwest Virginia.

In early February, 2003, we set out to do the Texas Bird Trail. During the interim, we had traded our trailer in on a 33 foot Sunnybrook fifth wheel trailer. We had also purchased a new Dodge dual wheel pickup with a diesel engine to pull it.

We made reservations for the month of March on South Padre Island. Our first stop was in east Texas where Ann saw many birds she had not seen before. We traveled down the Texas coast to Galveston, then turned inland to Choke Canyon State Park. This is a beautiful place with a lot of wildlife.

A few days after arrival, it turned cold and there was freezing rain all night. Shortly after we fixed breakfast, we ran out of propane. I went into town to have the tanks filled. At the propane station, there was a rancher killing time in the office. When he saw my Virginia tags, he asked, "What is a man from Virginia doing in Texas in the middle of winter?" I replied, "I am here as a driver and gopher. I drive my wife around for her to see the birds and go for whatever we need." Then he asked, "Has she seen the Arctic Snow Bank Tern." I replied, "I do not know. What does it look like?" Smiling, he said, "I am not sure what he looks like, but you can always recognize him by his call. He hides in a brush pile and calls, "Dammit, it's cold in south Texas in the wintertime." Everyone roared with laughter at the man's joke.

Later, on the way to South Padre, we stopped on the banks of the Rio Grande River. Ann was watching water birds. A vanload of students and a professor unloaded and began to join her in bird-watching. Soon, two young men from Mexico on the opposite bank took off their clothes, put them on top of their heads and waded across. All of the binoculars were turned on the waders. They were picked up by a man in an old car and quickly headed inland. (So much for border security.) Since I did not have binoculars out looking at birds, the professor asked who I was. My reply, "I am Ray and I am an S.O.B." and quickly added, "the spouse of a birder."

On the first of March, we checked in at a waterfront site on South Padre Island. Some of the campers were complaining that it was college spring break and the island was full of students. Since we had lived in two college towns, we rather enjoyed students. It is legal to drive on the beach there, but many kids tried to drive the family car on the beach and got stuck. At McDonald's, we ate breakfast with two agriculture students who had arrived in their father's four-wheel-drive farm pickup. They had a long chain and were pulling stuck cars out for $25 a tow.

When we left South Padre, we headed inland to San Antonio and then turned north to San Marcos. I wanted Ann to see Gary Air Force Base, where I went to helicopter school while in the Army. My time there was from April to August, 1956. Today, the base is a job corps training center. We reached home during the second week in April. Since our new trailer was larger than our earlier one, I had to expand the garage I had built to house it.

After a relaxing summer, we returned to Florida for the winter in October. Once there, I decided to turn my thoughts to writing again. My earlier books had both sold out the first printing, so I felt sure that there were some folks who would read a third book. Since high school, I had always enjoyed novels, and in college, I took an elective course on the English novel. Almost on a whim, I decided to write a novel. Before writing, I read a book by leading professors of creative writing. One of their themes was to write about what you know. I knew about soldiers, ministers, and India, so I started to write about a soldier-turned-preacher who went to India. The story became *Light From the East,* which is available from Publish America and Amazon, and as an e-book from Barnes and Noble and Amazon. I have started the sequel, which I hope to complete after this book is finished.

Since we were not doing an interim, we were free to attend the Sunnybrook International rallies and the Virginia chapter of the RV club. We enjoyed the group. Several asked me about our trip to Alaska, and we shared stories and pictures of our trip. A member suggested that we take an RV trip to Alaska in the summer of 2004 with them. We agreed, and the word soon got out about what we were planning. Many in the club said they wanted to go and by the time we were ready to depart, there were six couples. I had thought that when I stopped doing interims, it might be fun to lead RV caravans. This experience cured me of those thoughts. In the 18 months we had traveled nonstop together, Ann and I learned how to "overnight" and quickly get on the road the next morning. By this time, I could put my trailer anywhere I wanted to. We were comfortable dry camping, that is, without any hookups—simply using onboard water and holding tanks. Three of the couples did not handle this well. Things did not go as smoothly as planned, and three of the couples decided to go home early. In the end, this made the trip more enjoyable for the three couples who remained, and we traveled the entire summer as planned. I have led hundreds of travelers on international trips or mission trips, but I do not have the patience to lead RVers.

In November, 2006, we began an interim at Airlee Court Baptist Church in Roanoke. We were there on Sundays and Wednesdays. The church had an attendance of around 100. They were willing to call a person who had recently finished seminary. They called a young couple from Georgia. It looked like a good match. He came in early 2007.

On July 13, 2007, our children threw us a 50th anniversary party. We all decided that rather than have it be a formal occasion, we would rent a large picnic shelter at a nearby church. Our daughters decorated the tables with objects that reminded us of our 50 years together. Friends and family shared stories from their experiences with the two of us. We were able to move from table to table and visit with everyone that came. It was a grand affair, so much so that a couple who attended did their 50th the same way later in the year.

In the fall, we returned to Florida for the winter thinking it was time to end our second career of interim work. Our daughters and their families came and stayed the week after Christmas. It was a great week of fishing, swimming, and just being together. Ann Beth, our older daughter, who teaches special needs kindergartners, decided she wanted to take some things from Florida back for her students to see. One thing she had her sister bring back for her was a stalk of bananas. Unbeknownst to her, there was a small lizard that was using it as a home. The lizard (brown anole) decided he wanted to move to Virginia and hide in the banana stalk. He stayed concealed until Ann Beth took the stalk to her class. Then, he jumped down and made a mad dash, to the delight of the children. When he was finally caught, they put him in an aquarium and named him "Rocky." He could be released because of the cold winters in Virginia. He became rather famous after the local paper ran an article about the children and their lizard. Our daughter, Beth, kept us up-to-date on Rocky. Her reports were included in the Crooked Hook newsletter. When he died two years later, he was buried as a Virginian.

Both of my daughters are extremely dedicated to the children they teach. My younger daughter, Katie, along with her daughter, Katelyn, and I were eating lunch at McDonald's.

Katelyn and I decided we wanted some ice cream. When I went to the counter to order, the manager came from the back to serve me. When I tried to pay, he said, "It's on the house." I asked, "Why?" His response, "You are Mrs. Forbish's father, aren't you? I would never have finished high school and gotten into management if she had not been my teacher." Writing this brings tears to this proud father's eyes.

Meanwhile, we made plans for my final trip to India. I recruited Dr. Stockburger and Mrs. Tina Lee, a nurse from Blacksburg, to go with me. Dr. Stockburger accompanied me on many trips to India. He made a major contribution of time and money to the Indian Mission. Rodger Hogan (a pastor and youth minister at Airlee Court Baptist) and Jesse Taylor also agreed to go. Rodger was a retired police officer and Jesse, a convicted armed robber. The plan was to let them work in the prisons. They were both a tremendous success. Dr. Don Reid (who had been the missions pastor at Blacksburg) and his wife brought a group from the Fredericksburg area on the trip. Dr. Chris Monroe, the senior associate and worship leader for Vinton Baptist Church, and his wife, Mary Beth, also went. I met all of them in New York.

My major task on the trip was to be the graduation speaker. As we drove from the hotel, I could not help but remember those who had joined in the India effort, but had passed away: Dr. Joe Straughan, a physician from Wise, Virginia; Dr. Joe Strother, a pastor from Newport News, Virginia; Rev. Joe Burton, a pastor from Radford, Virginia; and at the time of this writing, Dr. Don Reid, who passed away at the young age of 58.

A hot, February day in India in 2007 was soon to be one of the proudest and yet, most humbling days of my life. The first place they took me was the library that they had named in my honor: the Dr. Ray Allen Library. My picture will hang there, along with the other founders of the seminary: Dr. Bill Ross and Dr. Kunjamon Chacko. Perhaps, just as I wondered about the men whose portraits hung on the wall at the University of Richmond, future students will wonder what we were like.

At the graduation, they crowned me king of the ceremonies. They presented me with a beautifully-carved cane saying that it was a shepherd's crook, because I had been the good shepherd to them for many years. This was so ironic, since I couldn't spell "shepherd" in college.

I spoke on the sixth chapter of Isaiah. I warned the students that some of them would go far in life and may even become famous. I told them to not be tempted to become the king's preacher, but always remember to be the preacher of the King of Kings.

After the ceremony, the students asked me to keep my doctoral robe and hood on, so that they could take pictures with me and their families. I felt honored and humbled to have my picture taken with these new ministers. After graduation, they would leave to go to all parts of India to share the love of Jesus. Today, students come from all parts of Asia to study at the India Baptist Theological Seminary.

That evening as I took off my clothes that were wet with perspiration, I remembered the day, years earlier, when Dr. John Upton and I laid the cornerstone for the seminary. At that time, we only had the bricks for the ceremony. Today, it is a beautiful campus. It stands because of the faith, dedication, and untiring work of Kunjamon Chacko, a most remarkable man. Dr. Upton is now the executive director of Virginia Baptist and the president of the Baptist World Alliance.

When the time came to pack for the trip home, I discovered my cane was too long to fit into my suitcase. It would not fit into any of the suitcases of the other members of the group, either. I certainly did not want to cut a piece off of it to make it fit. Then it occurred to me: "You are a gray-haired, old man. Walk with the cane." So that's what I did. Gray-haired, old men walking with canes get to board airplanes first. This made the trip home the easiest one I had ever had.

On the last leg of the journey, from New York to West Palm Beach, I traveled alone while my fellow travelers flew to Roanoke or Richmond. At 11:00 p.m., the flight attendants let me board first. As I flew down the east coast, I knew that this would be my last trip to India. The long flights in coach were becoming too much for my aging hips. The next day, I would turn a new page in life. I felt good about what had happened in India. There were over 100 students enrolled in the seminary. The children's homes were taking care of over 800 children. Younger men had stepped up to take my place. Virginia Baptists were winding down their partnership with India, but the Baptist Women were just beginning theirs. Bill Ross and Chris Monroe were providing great leadership and support for their work.

In March, 2008, the chairman of deacons at Airlee Court Baptist telephoned me and said that the young pastor they had called had resigned. He went back home to Georgia. He wanted me to return and do a second interim. I agreed to return April 1st, but only to stay until October 1st. When I returned, I found that some in the congregation had been very critical of the pastor and his wife, and that their leaving was not just a matter of their being homesick. We tried to address the issues.

Our younger daughter, Katie, and her husband, Larry, came over and taught the young married couples' class. The problem was that they and the two or three young couples who attended did not feel accepted by the congregation. I enjoyed having them there very much because Katelyn, their daughter, and I sat in the church office during Sunday school and talked. The church began a search for a new pastor and called a retired Army chaplain. I thought that he would be able to handle the dysfunction that was prevalent there. He resigned a few months after accepting the position.

When you end a stage in life, if you have been active and are in good health, you need to find something to fill up the days. If you have been blessed with meaningful work, then you want to continue to do things that have meaning. I had had the good fortune to serve on many boards and committees, but I had also seen too many people hang on to this, and in their old age, undo many of the worthwhile things that they had accomplished. Further, I felt that in their continuing to serve, they prevented a younger person from having the opportunity to serve. I was still getting opportunities to preach and teach in Virginia and Florida. I welcome these opportunities, and plan to continue as long as I do not put people to sleep.

The Religious Herald asked me to write an article about being an ordained minister for 50 years. When the article came out, it was well-received by their readers. Baptist Women and Virginia Baptist asked me to write a history of Virginia Baptist Partnership Missions. I first resisted because I knew there were better writers than I. Their response was that I was one of the few people still living who was involved from the beginning. After much reflection, I agreed and planned to use many stories from the volunteers. Gathering stories and researching the 30-year history took far more time than I imagined. My involvement had been more on the international side, so I recruited Roland Bailey, who had led the domestic side, to write about that. Finally, it all came together and was published by the Center for Baptist Heritage and Studies, University of Richmond, Virginia.

Arms Reaching Around the World was released in November, 2012 at the annual missions banquet. As nice things were said about me at the release, I honestly felt a little strange. Strange, because I knew that if any of my teachers was living, they would be surprised. For four years in a row, I flunked spelling in high school. Even in college, with the exception of the elective course I took on the English novel, I had never made more than a C in English. This was my fourth book and several thousand people had read my books. At that banquet, I decided to write my story and a sequel to *Light from the East*. Maybe my third career would be as a writer.

Meanwhile, I was enjoying more free time for my family and friends. My grandson, Michael, was coming every year to visit us in Florida and to fish. One day in the Everglades, he caught his first eight-pound bass. A year later, while fishing with me, his father, Dean caught his first eight-pound bass. Our son, Ray, Jr., and his son, Matthew, also love to come and fish with me. Matt holds the record for the largest catch. He caught a five-foot alligator, which his father filmed. His pictures were a tremendous hit with his third-grade class back in Richmond. The reader might wonder why, from time to time, I include a fish story. The reason is simple. Jesus liked fishermen.

Ann, who is not only into birds, but all kinds of wildlife, had always wanted to go to the Galapagos Islands. Frankly, I had not been very interested in that trip. In the fall of 2008, we made plans to go. We decided that this would be our last international trip, so we booked ourselves on a cruise specializing in travel for seniors. I decided to read Darwin's *Voyage of the Beagle* in preparation for the trip. It is a very interesting book. We arrived in Guayaquil, Ecuador, February 4, 2009. Since we knew little about South American history, I was surprised to learn that this city was founded before Jamestown or St. Augustine. It is a beautiful place with very friendly people. After a couple of days sightseeing, we caught a plane over to the islands. It was a fascinating experience. It turned out to be one of our best trips.

On these isolated islands, wildlife has developed into amazingly different species from the mainland. My conviction as a Christian is that God created the world through a process. The process is still going on. For all creatures, the process is the survival of the fittest. The process is pretty ruthless. Man has developed tools that prevent him from being subject to what we see in the wild. God created us to have dominion over the creation and to be good stewards of the planet. The first chapter of Genesis freed us from seeing the creation as being run by gods or demons that man needed to fear. With fear removed, we became free to study the creation and use what we learned for the betterment of ourselves and all the creatures of the planet. There is no conflict between honest science and honest religion. Science is about objectively studying the universe. It may take us back to the first grain of sand, but when one makes the judgment as to how it came about, he is making a faith judgment. In the beginning, God said, "Let there be…" and the process that became the universe began.

Perhaps this is a good place to bring my story to an end. In doing so, I would like to go back to the cane I received on my last trip to India. When I first received this gift, I thought that the only way to get it home was to find a way to fit it into a box, a suitcase. As I let go of the box, then the possibility of using it opened up a better trip for me. Our lives create boxes in which we condition ourselves to live. God is always calling us to think and walk outside the box. My early life created a box that I believed to be true—that I was not as smart or as talented as others. The army called me out of that. When I went to the University of Richmond, I still had vestiges of the dumb box, but Dr. Rhodenhiser called me out of that box, and helped me to use the good mind that God had given me. When I finished seminary, my box was to find a church like the people I had grown up with. Then, out of the box, God took me to Wise, a college town. In going to Cosby Memorial, I was, in some ways, returning to my roots. Then, in going to Blacksburg, God was calling me out of the box of my past forever. He never stops, because I became very comfortable living the comfortable life of a successful, university pastor. So He took me out of my comfortable box to mission work in India. God is forever calling us to leave our boxes of comfort and step out in faith to walk with Him.

How did my racket work out? It began in poverty, but became a life of being blessed far more than I could have ever imagined.

AFFIRMATION THEOLOGY

The summer of 1980 I was a visiting professor at the Southeastern Baptist Theological Seminary. I taught a large class of students the practical aspects of being a pastor. Their last written assignment was to write an essay on a successful pastor's theology. They had spent their years in school primarily studying the theology of professors, and I hoped they would understand that that those who work in churches also have a theology that undergirds their work. One student's essay was entitled *The Affirmation Theology of Dr. Ray Allen*. I had never named my personal theology. The student did an excellent job of describing my theology. Naturally he received an A plus for his essay. I wish I had saved a copy, but I did not. In conclusion I wish to share with my readers some reflections on the central idea that has unified my life and been the foundation of my leadership and ministry to people.

Most pastors are more inclined to preach and teach from the letters of Paul than they are from the Gospels. I was having lunch with a new Baptist minister in a sister church in Blacksburg. He commented, "I preach from Paul and use Jesus to illustrate." In Wise without thinking about it, I began to study and preach most of my sermons from of the gospels. Soon I saw that a great part of Jesus' success with people was he affirmed them and their God given potential.

He began his ministry by calling a group of fishermen and affirming they could become fishers of men. His first miracle was in response to a family who had suffered the embarrassment of running out of refreshments at their daughter's wedding. (John 2) At Jacob's well he reached out to a woman who had trouble staying married and offered to make her life a spring of living water. She could not worship in Samaria, where she lived, or in Jerusalem, so Jesus told her God had made a place for the likes of her. She could worship in truth and spirit anywhere. (John 4.7-24) The religious people brought him a woman caught in the act of adultery ready to stone her to death. Jesus reminded them of their own sin. Then he affirmed the potential within her with the words "Go and sin no more." Deep within, she felt the power of his belief in her that she could do it. His grace reinforced with the power of affirmation transformed her life. (John 8:1-11)

Peter denied Christ three times and cursed like the fisherman he had been. So deep in the depths of despair and shame, he went back to this fishing. Even that did not work for him anymore. He threw his net into the Sea of Galilee all night and caught nothing. In the morning mist, a man appears on the shore and shouts, "Throw your net on the other side." In an act of blind faith, he throws. The net overflows. He recognizes only one person he has ever known has the power to fill his empty net. With his head tucked in shame, he comes ashore. Three times Jesus questions him, "Do you love me?" Three times Peter responds, each time lowering his head even more. Three times Jesus affirms his faith in Peter with the challenge, "Feed my flock." Peter you are my man. I put you in charge. I am entrusting you with the leadership of my church. (John 21:1-19) It was next to impossible for Peter not to accept the forgiveness Jesus offered and the faith Jesus placed in him. In

God's grace and Jesus affirmation all things became possible for Peter. On Easter Sunday the believers announced he is risen which we proclaim to this day. The risen Christ announced I believe in these simple fishermen. I trust them to found my church and change the world. They, in fact, did not fail the faith placed in them.

When anyone places his faith in Christ, the angels in heaven rejoice. That believer is adopted into the family of God. Their baptismal certificate is their birth certificate. It may be hard for you to believe, but like the early believers our honest profession may well be. "I believe, Oh Lord, help my unbelief." If we accept the second miracle of faith which is God believes in you as one of his children by committing ourselves to him, our God given potential can be born and flourish whether it is one talent or five. This is God's gift of grace and power to all who believe his affirmation of us.

This is a most powerful gift we can give to each other. This is not blindly looking at others and denying we are all forgiven sinners each with a unique set of problems, but it is seeing we all are uniquely made with a God given talent and potential. It is affirming this when the other person may be in a sea of self-doubt. It was what my wife Ann did when she married me a young soldier with so little money I had to ask her for gas money to get back to the base. It is what Dr. Hackley did when after 50 years of teaching said to my first class in Latin, "I have looked at your records; you are the best class I ever taught, I would not be surprised if you all made A." It was what Dr. Bill Rhodenhiser did when he called me aside and told me my answers were excellent in class, but I needed to learn to write them down. It was what Walter Johnson's Sunday school class did with their letters of encouragement and gifts of money during my years of seminary. It was what Dr. Dale Moody did when he told me even though I would not be staying to study more with him, he said he was going to find me a good church. It was what the Wise Baptist Church did when they accepted and loved an inexperienced young minister and his family and showed it by showering us with praise. A member of my Sunday School Class last Sunday put it well when said he hoped to be the man his dog thought he was.

Life has taught me that there is power in blessing others by affirming them and believing in them. This not only blesses them, but blesses us as well. If a pastor loves, believes in his people, and affirms them, many will love, affirm him and follow his leadership. Together they may well achieve things they never thought possible

THE FAMILY AND HOW IT WORKED OUT.

My favorite professor in seminary often said, "Fellows, if you fail family, you fail in ministry regardless of how successful you might be. So I want to share with my readers how our family worked out because they are what I am most proud of. First when Ann and I started out as two 19 year old kids with almost no money and from such different backgrounds, the cards of life were stacked against us. Yet through better and worse, we hung in there and after 56 years of marriage still love each other deeply and far more maturely. Staying married is a great challenge in today's world, but it is worth the effort. I am equally proud that our children made fine choices in choosing their spouses. They have all remained married and are active in their churches.

Our oldest, Ann Elizabeth Allen Cranwell, is an elementary special education teacher. Her husband of 33 years, Dean, is a health care attorney. Their son, Michael, is married to Danielle. He is a health care administrator, and she a customer service representative in commercial insurance at a bank. Dean and Ann's daughter, Rebecca is a copy writer for an internet company, and a freelance writer.

Ray Allen, Jr., owns a political consulting firm in Richmond and is a partner or owner of several other businesses. His wife of 22 years, Melinda, works in their business. Their daughter,

Jennifer, is an honor student in her junior year of high school. Their son, Matthew, is an honor middle school student.

Our daughter, Kathleen (Katie) Johnson Allen Forbish is a high school English teacher. Her husband, Larry, of 25 years is an investment counselor and a bank officer. Their daughter, Katelyn, is a dean's list student and a sophomore at Virginia Tech. She is studying print and multi-media communications.

All three of our children are in fields where they are trying to make the world we live in a better place. Rarely do I eat out that some student of my two daughters does not come and tell me how they helped them in school. Few places do I go in our state when someone fails to ask what relationship am I to Ray Allen, Jr. Once they were being asked are your kin to the pastor of Baptist Church? Now it is reversed. I am recognized by their lives' work. How is it possible for an old man to be any more blessed than to have his children recognized at the city gates?

Thank you, Lord!

AVAILABILITY OF RAY ALLEN'S BOOKS

How to Be a Christian, Happy and Successful Amazon. Com

Our Common Faith Amazon. Com

Light from the East PublishAmerica. Com, Amazon and Barnes and Noble

Arms Reaching Around the World
The Center for Baptist Heritage and Studies Box 34
University of Richmond, VA 23179

CPSIA information can be obtained at www.ICGtesting.com
Printed in the USA
BVOW01s0555300414

352073BV00001B/4/P